In this important collection of spiritual reflections, Monsignor Francis Kelly provides a valuable resource whereby we can establish or further develop a sense of the sacred in our lives. In the face of the increasingly hectic pace of daily life we need a prompting to help us pause and rediscover the presence of the Lord. *Through the Church Year: Reflections for Feasts and Seasons* provides such help for us, through an engaging and accessible guide for the liturgical seasons and the major solemnities and feast days of the saints. We are blessed to have such a helpful resource available to us. I highly recommend this book to all who seek to live their faith more fully and gain greater insight into the beauty of the Church.

**Cardinal Séan O'Malley, O.F.M. Cap.**
Archbishop of Boston

Growing up in a wonderful parish and Catholic grade school, I often remember the pastor and the sisters telling us that "The feasts and seasons of the Church year are the best teacher of faith we have." Monsignor Kelly's helpful and rewarding book shows the wisdom of that childhood lesson.

**Most Reverend Timothy M. Dolan**
Archbishop of New York

Monsignor Kelly is an accomplished writer and expert catechi.. this book, he demonstrates his ability to communicate both the beauty and the wisdom of the major celebrations of the liturgical year. It is a pleasure for me to recommend *Through the Church Year* in the hope that all who use it will find in it a strengthening of their faith and a renewal of their appreciation for the beauty of the liturgy.

**Most Reverend Donald W. Wuerl, S.T.D.**
Archbishop of Washington

Born of prayerful reflection on the readings and prayers of the church's liturgy, this book is a pastoral gem. It is an important synthesis of historical information, biblical commentary, and wise use of classical and contemporary authors to help uncover the richness of the church's "spiritual director"—the liturgy. It will be of enormous benefit for anyone seeking a deeper appreciation of feasts and seasons. Highly recommended for all who want to celebrate the liturgy with greater insight and knowledge.

**Rev. Msgr. Kevin W. Irwin, S.T.D.**
Dean, School of Theology and Religious Studies
Catholic University of America

Monsignor Kelly's *Through the Church Year* provides a helpful tool for understanding the riches of the liturgical year. It is a good companion on the journey of faith leading one to dwell more deeply at the heart of the Church.

**Donna Orsuto**
Professor, Pontifical Gregorian University
Director, The Lay Centre at Foyer Unitas

In this new book, Monsignor Kelly shares the fruit of a long priestly contemplation. He places the mysteries of Christ, of Our Lady, and of the saints within reach of those Catholics who seek to discover in the annual celebration of feast days a source of personal support for daily Christian living. Monsignor Kelly both informs and edifies.

**Romanus Cessario, O.P.**
Saint John's Seminary, Boston, Massachusetts
Senior Editor of MAGNIFICAT®

The prime intent of Monsignor Kelly's handy volume is to help the reader live the Church's liturgical year spiritually and profitably. This volume is ideal for prayer, such as *lectio divina*, and priests will find within its pages seeds for homilies. This volume is a *vade mecum* for anyone who has interest in liturgical spirituality.

**Joseph N. Tylenda, S.J.**
Author of *Saints and Feasts of the Liturgical Year*

*Through the Church Year* is a work of spiritual pedagogy. By balancing history, reflections, and liturgical commentary, Monsignor Kelly offers the reader an inspiring compendium on the Liturgical Year. These pages both educate and inspire.

**(Reverend) Gregory J. Hoppough, C.S.S., S.T.D.**
Professor of Liturgical Studies
Blessed John XXIII National Seminary, Weston, Massachusetts

# Through the Church Year

## Reflections for Feasts and Seasons

### Francis D. Kelly

ave maria press AmP notre dame, indiana

---

Founded in 1865, Ave Maria Press is a ministry of the Indiana Province of Holy Cross.

www.avemariapress.com

ISBN-10 1-59471-174-7  ISBN-13 978-1-59471-174-9

Cover image © age fotostock/Superstock.

Cover and text design by Katherine Robinson Coleman.

Printed and bound in the United States of America.

*Library of Congress Cataloging-in-Publication Data*

Kelly, Francis D.
  Through the church year : reflections for feasts and seasons / Francis D. Kelly.
  p. cm.
  Includes bibliographical references.
  ISBN-13: 978-1-59471-174-9 (pbk.)
  ISBN-10: 1-59471-174-7 (pbk.)
  1. Church year meditations. 2. Catholic Church—Prayers and devotions.  I. Title.
BX2170.C55K45 2009
242'.3—dc22
                                                      2009015460

# Contents

# $\mathcal{I}$ntroduction

❖

One of the Holy Spirit's great gifts to the Church, Christ's Bride, is the sacred liturgy, including the liturgical year with its weekly Sunday celebration, its seasons, solemnities, and feasts. This is one of the primary ways the Spirit draws us more deeply into the mystery of Christ, that we might be more conformed to his likeness and so grow in holiness, and in love and service for our brothers and sisters. There were many periods of the Church's history in which the celebration of the liturgical year was the chief means of transmission of the faith and of catechizing people about the mystery of salvation in Christ. The adage *lex orandi, lex credendi*—how we pray shows what we believe—is relevant here.

The frenetic pace of modern life, including the bombardment of our senses by the cacophony of the media, does not easily lend itself to recollection or a taste for "mystery" beyond our senses. Precisely for this reason, a rediscovery of the Church's rhythms of prayer and worship can be a powerful aid in deepening our Christian life. The proper observance of Sundays, solemnities, feasts, and seasons helps us to live our lives more consciously in God's presence.

This book is a modest effort to be of assistance to those who wish to explore more deeply the value of liturgical spirituality and thereby infuse their lives with the presence and grace of Christ. The renewal of the Church's liturgy launched by the Second Vatican Council helped make a liturgical spirituality more possible and accessible to many. The council highlighted the priority and centrality of the sacred liturgy:

> Every liturgical celebration, because it is an action of Christ the Priest and of his Body, which is the Church, is a sacred action surpassing all others. No other action of the Church can equal its efficacy. (*Sacrosanctum Concilium*, 7)

The council launched the most thorough reform in liturgy the Church has ever known. The goal of this reform was the "full and active participation of the faithful" in the liturgy—rescuing it from being a ritual performed by the priest alone while the attendees perhaps pursued their personal devotions. Liturgical spirituality therefore draws us all into the great ever-present work of Christ the Priest: leading God's People in prayer, adoration, and thanksgiving to God the Father, with the consequent transforming effects for our lives.

Liturgical spirituality encourages us to make the eucharist, which the council calls "the summit and source of the Christian life" (*Sacrosanctum Concilium*, 10), truly the highlight of our own personal lives, with daily participation where possible. It also invites us to share in the Church's life of daily prayer by use of the liturgy of the hours, especially consecrating our day by praying morning and evening prayer with the Church.

# Sundays

Every Sunday is a special day of grace focused on the remembrance of the Paschal Mystery of Jesus' death and resurrection. It is the weekly celebration of the victory of light over darkness, grace over sin, life over death. This observance thus has great relevance for our lives and is a source of renewed hope each week. In his apostolic letter *Dies Domini* (The Day of the Lord), Pope John Paul II writes:

> In commemorating the day of Christ's Resurrection not just once a year but every Sunday, the Church seeks to indicate to every generation the true fulcrum of history, to which the mystery of the world's origin and its final destiny leads.
>
> It is right, therefore, to claim, in the words of a fourth century homily, that "the Lord's Day" is "the lord of days." Those who have received the grace of faith in the Risen Lord cannot fail to grasp the significance of this day of the week with the same deep emotion which led Saint Jerome to say: "Sunday is the day of the Resurrection, it is the day of Christians, it is our day." For Christians, Sunday is "the fundamental feast day," established not only to mark succession of time but to reveal time's deeper meaning. (*Dies Domini*, 2)

In the past, Catholics typically observed Sunday as a holy day, but in our secularized society it has became a day for shopping, sports, and other secular activities. The recapturing of Sunday as a day of prayer and worship and family relaxation and celebration needs to be a pastoral priority. Cardinal John Henry Newman expressed this eloquently:

> One important benefit arising from the institution of the Lord's Day for Christians busied about many things—it reminds them of the one thing needful and keeps them from being drawn into the great whirlpool of time and sense.

Most men feel wearied with the dust of this world when Saturday comes and understand it to be a mercy that they are not obliged to go on toiling without cessation . . . the weekly Services of prayer and praise come to us as a gracious relief, a pause from the world, a glimpse of the third heaven, lest the world should rob us of our hope, and enslave us to that hard master who is plotting our eternal destruction. (*Parochial and Plain Sermons*, Book III, Sermon 23)

As a practical spiritual benefit from Sunday, it should be noted that the Church in ordinary time surrounds the Sunday liturgy with a continuous reading of the synoptic gospels of Matthew, Mark, and Luke. This is a wonderful way for individuals and families to enter into the message of the Lord by reflecting on and discussing together the content of these gospels, perhaps with the help of appropriate commentaries.

## Seasons, Solemnities, and Feasts

In addition to Sunday, the liturgical year is structured around the great seasons—Advent, Christmastide, Lent, Eastertide—which present to us anew the mystery of Christ in all its fullness so that each aspect may be worshiped and give to us its unique grace. Our lives change—we are always at a different point in our life journey with new challenges and new needs. God is always at work in our lives doing wonderful things! Our observance of these special seasons each year helps us to relate every moment of our life journey to the power of Christ's mystery that endures and is truly accessible to us.

The joyful expectation of Advent, the consoling presence of Emmanuel at Christmas, the lenten challenge to conversion and transformation, the Easter experience of the power of Christ's grace, the Pentecostal celebration of the Spirit's coming—all are woven each year into the fabric of our personal life's journey at whatever stage we find ourselves, and they transform and sanctify it.

It is also remarkable how wonderfully the liturgical season—at least in the Northern Hemisphere—harmonizes with and complements the seasons of nature! The dark of winter is pierced by the birth of Christ—"the light of the world." Spring's rebirth of nature is mirrored in the new life that comes to Christians by their lenten efforts at self-renewal crowned by the grace of the risen Christ. The fiery coming of the Spirit at the beginning of summer inspires us to vibrantly witness to Christ, just as it inspired the apostles to do the same at Pentecost.

Finally, the solemnities and feasts of the Church year provide a special opportunity to focus on and celebrate a specific mystery of Christ, a privilege of his Mother Mary, or the witness of some saint. They are landmarks of grace and celebration throughout the year.

## Through the Church Year

In this book I have attempted to be of service by providing a brief historical note for many of these observances—seasons, solemnities, and feasts—and offering some reflections for prayerful meditation. Some of these reflections may be useful catalysts for homilies, but primarily this book is intended as a resource for personal prayer and spiritual growth.

The reflections of this book are the fruit of a lifetime of joyful and grateful participation in these holy mysteries and sacred times. Over the years the author has garnered from saints, popes, and theologians insights and graces in his own attempt to observe the Church year. In this book, these are now ordered and arranged so that they might be helpful to others as a way of fulfilling the injunction of St. Thomas Aquinas: *contemplata aliis tradere,* "share with others the fruit of contemplation."

One cannot observe seriously the liturgical year without becoming aware that it is really one continuous "love story"—the incredible merciful love of the Creator God for his creatures. At each stage of the year a different aspect of that love is manifested. In the meditations that follow, therefore, the author hopes to lead the reader to an ever deeper wonder at the awesome love of God and to a response to that love in which "there is no fear" (1 Jn 4:18).

There is a genre of literature of this kind that has helped many. One thinks especially of Abbot Prosper Gueranger's *L'Annee Liturgique* and Fr. Pius Parsch's *Year of Grace*. This volume is a very humble effort to follow in that stream of liturgical devotion.

The author has been singularly blessed, over the course of his lifetime, to have been able to share in the celebration of the liturgical year with a number of monastic communities. This work is gratefully dedicated to some of those—especially St. Joseph's Cistercian Abbey in Spencer, Massachusetts; St. Anselm's Benedictine Abbey in Manchester, New Hampshire; Holy Cross Cistercian Abbey in Berryville, Virginia; St. Benedict's Benedictine Abbey in Still River, Massachusetts; and the Cistercian Abbey of Tre Fontane in Rome. The prayer and the example of these communities and others has been a great grace, and the author gratefully acknowledges their hospitality and spiritual support.

May Mary, the model of contemplative prayer, who "kept all these things in her heart" (Lk 2:51), intercede that this effort may be a source of grace and help to many.

Rome, 2008

# $\mathcal{A}$dvent

---

✤

## Historical Background

---

Lent-Easter-Pentecost is the chief focus of the liturgical year and historically its oldest element. This sequence celebrates the Paschal Mystery of our salvation by the death and rising of Jesus, Our Lord.

A second important focus of the Church year is "the celebration and expectation of the coming of Christ, a theme extended in current western liturgical practice over the many weeks that comprise the Advent-Christmas-Epiphany cycle."[1]

Advent is focused on the various comings of the Redeemer. The first Sunday especially focuses on the final Parousia—Christ's glorious coming at the end of time. The second and third Sundays highlight John the Baptist's heralding of Christ's earthly coming. The fourth and final Sunday concerns itself with the immediate historical preludes to Jesus' birth. In the four weeks of Advent, therefore, the meaning of the coming of the Messiah shifts from the expectation of the consummation of history itself to preparation for the Nativity of the Savior.

The development of the Advent season in the Church's year was gradual; it seems to have had its beginnings in the fourth century:

> While we may be sure that the Advent season developed first outside of Rome, to say more than that is not as easy as one might wish. . . . A canon of the Council of Saragozza (Spain) in 380 urges the constant presence of the faithful in church during a period of twenty-one continuous days, beginning from December 17 and reaching to Epiphany.[2]

This may help explain our current practice of a more intensive preparation for Christmas from December 17 with the praying of the O Antiphons. It is significant that those dates of December 17–23 also corresponded with the dates of a popular pagan festival, the Saturnalia, which the pastors of the ancient Church may have been trying to counteract. Interestingly, in later centuries Advent was longer than the current four-week season: seventh- and eighth-century Missals provide for six Sundays of Advent.

Above all, at Advent the Church wishes to focus the faithful on the Christ-Event, the appearance in our midst of the Incarnate Son of God, first humbly at Bethlehem and then at the end of time in glory to complete his saving work for the human family. Advent then is a joyful season, full of the expectation of these various comings of our Redeemer by which he manifests his boundless love for his creatures.

Reflections

---

## I.

*"I will raise up for David a just shoot."*
*(Jer 33:15)*

The dominant motif of this beautiful season can be captured in three words: promise, hope, and expectation. We read in this season's liturgies the ancient promises and prophecies of salvation in the Old Testament, especially from the Prophet Isaiah. We do this in order to rekindle our hope in the faithfulness of God, who realized many of these promises in the first coming of Christ and will bring them to a glorious fulfillment in the second coming of Christ in glory at the end of time.

Promise was a keynote of Israelite faith. No matter how often the people of God were unfaithful, God always held out hope for salvation. This promise and hope was especially focused on a descendant of King David:

> In those days, in that time, I will raise up for David a
> just shoot; he shall do what is right and just in the land.
> In those days Judah shall be safe. (Jer 33:15–16)

Even when Jerusalem was under siege or destroyed, and the people were brought into captive slavery, their trust in God's faithfulness and his promise of a Messiah endured:

> Bethlehem . . .

> From you shall come forth for me
> one who is to be ruler in Israel;
> Whose origin is from of old,
> from ancient times.
> (Therefore the Lord will give them up, until the time
> when she who is to give birth has borne. . . .)
> He shall stand firm and shepherd his flock

by the strength of the LORD,
in the majestic name of the LORD, his God;
And they shall remain, for now his greatness
shall reach the ends of the earth;
he shall be peace. (Mi 5:1–4)

Devout Jews preserved these hopes and expectations, and their faith nourishes ours, as we re-read so many of these promises in this special season when we prepare again to celebrate the birth of Christ.

## 2.

*"We also await a savior, the Lord Jesus Christ." (Phil 3:20)*

Christ was the fulfillment of God's promises to Israel. The angel Gabriel told Mary that her son "will rule over the house of Jacob forever, and of his kingdom there will be no end" (Lk 1:33). He was the true Messianic King. As always is the case in God's dealing with us, the realization far exceeded the expectation. The Messiah was not just a royal descendant of King David, but the very Son of God come as Universal Savior.

Jesus' humble existence and his ministry were an initial fulfillment of all these promises, but he promised a yet greater fulfillment when at the end of time he would return in power and glory to bring the Father's plan for history to its final fulfillment. He predicted: "they will see the Son of Man coming in a cloud with power and great glory" (Lk 21:27).

The first Christians lived by these promises and this expectation. As Paul wrote in one of the earliest books of the New Testament:

> You turned to God from idols to serve the living and true God and to await his Son from heaven, whom he raised from [the] dead, Jesus, who delivers us from the coming wrath. (1 Thes 1:9–10)

A frequent prayer of early Christians was "Come Lord Jesus." The New Testament even preserves it in the Aramaic language in which they prayed it: *Marana tha* (1 Cor 16:22). Earnestly they looked for Jesus' return:

> We also await a savior, the Lord Jesus Christ. He will change our lowly body to conform with his glorified body by the power that enables him also to bring all things into subjection to himself. (Phil 3:20–21)

## 3.

*"Beware that your hearts do not become drowsy."*
*(Lk 21:34)*

Unfortunately, with the passage of time the expectant spirit of the earliest Christians diminished. St. Luke saw it already in the churches to whom he ministered, warning them in the Lord's words:

> Beware that your hearts do not become drowsy from carousing and drunkenness and the anxieties of daily life, and that day catch you by surprise like a trap.... Be vigilant at all times and pray that you have the strength to escape the tribulations that are imminent and to stand before the Son of Man. (Lk 21:34–36)

The Advent season is a call for us to renew this sense of hopeful expectation. It is perhaps the spark that modern evangelization needs in order to enkindle a sense of confidence and enthusiasm for the good news of Jesus Christ.

It is sad that too many Christians settle down into a more or less morose, cynical, depressed attitude that is far from the spirit of the early Church. Their attitude is perhaps best expressed in the comment, "Blessed are those who expect nothing—they will not be disappointed." True Christians live in constant expectation and know that the realization of God's promises will always exceed all of our expectations.

One modern prophetic voice has eloquently expressed the need for a revival of our Advent hope:

> Expectation has never ceased to guide the progress of our faith like a torch. The Israelites were constantly expectant, and the first Christians too. Christmas, which might have been thought to turn our gaze towards the past, has only fixed it further in the future. The Messiah, who appeared for a moment in our midst, only allowed himself to be seen and touched for a moment before vanishing once again, more luminous and ineffable than ever, into the depths of the future. He came. Yet now we must expect him—no longer a small chosen group among us, but all men—once again and more then ever. The Lord Jesus will only come soon if we ardently expect him. It is an accumulation of desire that should cause the Pleroma to burst upon us. Successors to Israel, we Christians have been charged with keeping the flame of the desire ever alive in the world. Only twenty centuries have passed since the Ascension. What have we made of our expectancy? A certain pessimism, perhaps encouraged by an exaggerated conception of the original fall, has led us to regard the world as decidedly and incorrigibly wicked. And so we have allowed the flame to die down in our sleeping hearts. We persist in saying that we keep vigil in expectation of the Master. But in reality we should have to admit, if we were sincere, that we no longer expect anything. The flame must be revived at all costs. At all costs we must renew in ourselves the desire and the hope for the great Coming.[3]

# $\mathcal{I}$mmaculate Conception of Mary

## DECEMBER 8

✣

## Historical Background

The earliest Church, as reflected in the liturgies of the Eastern Church, instinctively honored Mary as "all holy," "all pure," "immaculate." This recognition expresses the truth already proclaimed in the New Testament when the angel Gabriel greeted Mary as "full of grace" (Lk 1:28).

After the doctrine of original sin was more fully developed in the fourth century, it became common to link Mary's fullness of grace to the very moment of conception; original sin never stained her soul. In the promulgation of the dogma of the Immaculate Conception by Blessed Pius IX in 1854, the Church definitively expressed its confidence in this fullness of grace given to Mary to render her worthy to be the very tabernacle of the Eternal Son. As if to give a heavenly endorsement of the dogma, when Our Lady appeared to St. Bernadette at Lourdes in 1858 she identified herself to Bernadette with these words: "I am the Immaculate Conception."

A feast of the Conception of Mary is documented in the East by the seventh century, and it passed into the West by 1100. It was approved for the whole Church by Innocent XII in 1695.[1] In 1846 the bishops of the United States chose Mary, under the title of the Immaculate Conception, as patroness of the United States. For this reason the great National Shrine Basilica of the Immaculate Conception was constructed in Washington, D.C.; it is the seventh largest church in the world.

Reflections

---

I.

*"You are all beautiful, O Mary, and there is no stain of original sin in you."*

This refrain from today's Divine Office expresses the Church's loving devotion to the Mother of God that we wish to echo with the Church all over the world. The English poet Wordsworth expressed this doctrine properly when he referred to Mary as "our tainted human nature's solitary boast." She is indeed, through God's great mercy, a mystery of sinless life. All this was possible, of course, only through the foreseen merits of Jesus Christ, the only Savior. This favor of the Immaculate Conception, being conceived in a fullness of grace, was granted to Mary with a view to her, role as Mother of the Divine Son. Fittingly, then, in the Advent season does the Church's spotlight of faith focus on her, who bears the Divine Savior to the human race. She is the "house of gold," the "ark of the Most High," the "Mother blest." Of this mystery, St. Ambrose of Milan (AD 340–97) writes:

It is not surprising that the Lord, having begun to redeem the world, should have begun his work with Mary: if salvation for all men was being prepared through her, she should be the first to obtain the fruit of salvation from her Son. (*Commentary on Luke*)

In a similar vein St. Augustine (AD 354–430) writes:

When there is talk of sin she must not even be mentioned, out of regard for the Lord. How could we ever know the immense gift of grace that pervaded her in order to safeguard her from all trace of sin, she who was worthy of conceiving and giving birth to him who had absolutely no sin? (*Treatise on Nature and Grace*, Ch. 36, 42)

This special grace, far from distancing Mary from us, unites her to us. She too is a member of the Church, the community of those redeemed by Christ. The Second Vatican Council expresses this paradoxical truth in its Dogmatic Constitution on the Church:

Because of this gift of sublime grace she far surpasses all creatures, both in heaven and on earth. But, being of the race of Adam, she is at the same time also united to all those who are to be saved; indeed, "she is clearly the mother of the members of Christ . . . since she has by her charity joined in bringing about the birth of believers in the Church, who are members of its head." Wherefore, she is hailed as pre-eminent and as a wholly unique member of the Church, and as its type and outstanding model in faith and charity. . . . The Catholic Church, taught by the Holy Spirit, honors her with filial affection and devotion as a most beloved mother. (*Lumen Gentium*, 53; the internal quote is from St. Augustine)

## 2.

*"Sing to the Lord a new song, / for he has done wondrous deeds."*
*(Ps 98:1)*

Today is the "feast of grace," not only because of Our Lady's plenitude of grace, but also because this day highlights the wider mystery of God's overflowing goodness and love for all his human creatures of whom Mary is the paramount example. "God is love" (1 Jn 4:16) and he pours out this love on us. In this way, in the second reading at today's Mass, Paul observes that it was "in love" that the Father destined us for adoption to himself through Jesus Christ, for the "praise of the glory of his grace that he granted us in the beloved [Jesus]" (Eph 1:6).

Christian anthropology, however, tells us that while God created everything good and created humankind in his friendship, the first humans, Adam and Eve, used their free will to rebel and disobey. The whole sad story is narrated in today's first reading at Mass from chapter 3 of Genesis. But God's love is so great that he would not allow his dream for humans to be thwarted. Human sin does not alter the plan and will of God who "chose us in [Christ], before the foundation of the world, to be holy and without blemish before him" (Eph 1:4). God found a remedy by sending his Son to reverse Adam's pride, disobedience, and sin and to unlock the floodgates of divine grace. This was all pure divine gift!

> The gift is not like the transgression. For if by that one person's transgression the many died, how much more did the grace of God and the gracious gift of the one person Jesus Christ overflow for the many. . . . For if, by the transgression of one person, death came to reign through that one, how much more will those who receive the abundance of grace and of the gift of justification come to reign in life through the one person Jesus Christ. (Rom 5:15–17)

God is Infinite Goodness; his plan and will are for our salvation and deification. His love is boundless and it is all sheer gift, pure grace. On this day we rejoice and entrust ourselves to this mystery of grace. Fittingly, the Responsorial Psalm today prays:

> Sing to the LORD a new song,
> for he has done wondrous deeds. . . .
> He has remembered his kindness and his
> faithfulness. . . .
> Sing joyfully to the LORD, all you lands;
> break into song; sing praise. (Ps 98:1, 3a, 4)

This "gift of grace" comes at a great price, as Pope John Paul II noted in his 1990 homily on this feast:

> We know the price paid by Jesus, the Son of Mary, our Savior. We know "we have been bought at a great price" (1 Cor 6:20). The Cross of Christ stands at the center of salvation history, at the center of human history as the sign of victory, of grace. Mary will stand beneath the Cross.

## 3.

*"May it be done to me according to your word." (Lk 1:38)*

What does it mean to "live in God's grace"? A model of a life lived "in grace" is offered to us by Mary, and we see an important event in her grace-filled life in today's gospel reading (Lk 1:26–38). Hers is a life rooted in God's love and in total trust in his goodness and grace. It is a life that is fully convinced that "nothing will be impossible for God" (Lk 1:37). In today's gospel Mary may seem to be at the center, but if we read more carefully we see that God is at the center. God is revealing his love and his will to Mary. She is the model of the person of faith: she listens, accepts, and surrenders her will into God's hands. She says her *fiat*, her "yes," without reserve: "May it be done to me according to your word" (Lk 1:38).

Mary is the model of the Church at its deepest level. While offices and structures in the Church (sometimes called the "Petrine charism") are essential and important, they are at the service of another charism, the Marian charism. That is, the Church and we who live the mystery of the Church must be like Mary, listening to the Word of God, docile, humble, obedient to God's will, surrendering ourselves to his plan, doing our part to bring Christ's salvation to the world. Let us turn to her on this day which celebrates her holiness and learn from her how truly to "live in the state of grace."

> O Mary Mother of Jesus and our mother help us to become open to the same omnipotence and the same power of love that made you so fruitful and so pleasing to God. Prepare us not only to listen, but to consent to the Lord, to accept willingly the unique call which is addressed to each one of us. Help us to become holy and blameless, full of love as we serve Jesus in our brothers and sisters all the days of our life. Help us to prepare a world for your Son.[2]

# $\mathcal{O}$ur Lady of Guadalupe

## DECEMBER 1 2

❧

## Historical Background

On this day in 1521, Juan Diego, an Amerindian layman, was favored with an apparition of Our Lady on Tepeyac Hill, near Mexico City. He was instructed to collect roses and bring them to the bishop with a request that a church be built. As he opened his tilma cloak to present the roses to the bishop, an image of Our Lady was seen on the cloak. In the image, Our Lady appears as a young girl with native features and dress, standing with hands clasped together in prayer.

Juan Diego's tilma has been venerated ever since in a great basilica near the site of the apparition. The tilma has been subjected to scientific analyses by several organizations, including the Kodak Company, and has been found to defy natural explanation both in terms of how it was painted and how it has remained preserved. To the eyes of faith, it is a beautiful gift from Our Lady to her children of the New World.[1]

## Reflections

---

### I.

*"As a mother comforts her son, / so will I comfort you."*
*(Is 66:13)*

"Am I not your Mother?" These tender and reassuring words of Our Lady to Juan Diego capture the spirit of the devotion to Our Lady of Guadalupe. She made herself known to the poor and oppressed in that country and said she wanted a church where her "love, compassion, and protection" could be invoked. The Mexican people have felt this special maternal care of Mary over the centuries and millions visit the Shrine of Guadalupe every year.

Mary's maternal love, however, is a gift for all people. She is truly the "Mother of Mercy" to whom all can turn in their needs and troubles. Mary's "fullness of grace," which we just celebrated on December 8, is expressed in a "fullness of love" for all God's children. Rooted in God, she shares his compassionate love for all of us. Her words quoted above speak to us a message of tenderness and kindness, of security and protection. They remind us of God's words in sacred scripture: "As a mother comforts her son, / so will I comfort you" (Is 66:13).

Mary's spiritual motherhood of all was precisely the aspect that Pope John Paul II highlighted in his address in 1982 on the 450th anniversary of the apparitions. He said:

> Mary's spiritual motherhood of all men is an aspect closely united with her divine motherhood. In fact, there appears right from the beginning in Guadalupan

devotion this characteristic feature, which pastors have always instilled and the faithful have lived with staunch trust. It is a feature learned by contemplating Mary in her extraordinary role in the mystery of the Church, stemming from her mission as the Savior's Mother. Precisely because she agrees to collaborate freely in God's saving plan, she participates actively, together with her Son, in the work of man's salvation. The Second Vatican Council expresses itself luminously about this function: "She conceived, brought forth, and nourished Christ, she presented him to the Father in the temple, shared her Son's sufferings as he died on the cross. Thus, in a wholly singular way she cooperated by her obedience, faith, hope, and burning charity in the work of the Savior in restoring supernatural life to the soul. For this reason she is mother to us in the order of grace" (*Lumen Gentium,* 61). It is a teaching that, pointing out the Blessed Virgin's cooperation in restoring the supernatural life of souls, speaks of her mission as the spiritual mother of men. Therefore the Church pays her the tribute of ardent love "when she considers the spiritual motherhood of Mary for all the members of the Mystical Body"(*Marialis Cultus,* 22). In this same line of teaching, Pope Paul VI will constantly declare Mary "Mother of the Church."[2]

These are not just abstract theological truths; rather, in our own spiritual life there should be a strong filial trust in Our Lady's maternal care that brings us serenity, peace, and confidence. This is the testimony and the witness of so many saints down through the centuries. May this special Advent feast be an occasion for us to renew this grace for ourselves and place ourselves more consciously under Mary's maternal care.

## 2.

*"Behold, I am the handmaid of the Lord. May it be done to me*
*according to your word." (Lk 1:38)*

It is significant that in the Guadalupe icon, Mary is presented as a "woman of prayer." She appears with hands folded
in devotion, eyes downcast in an atmosphere of recollection, peace, and surrender, echoing her basic prayer:
"Behold, I am the handmaid of the Lord. May it be done to
me according to your word"(Lk 1:38).

Could it be that with this image left on the tilma of Juan
Diego she wished to leave us a message, an invitation for
the deepening of our lives of prayer? It is certainly in harmony with the other well-known apparitions, for example,
Lourdes and Fatima, where Mary herself appears at prayer
and encourages the visionaries to be more serious about
prayer.

In the New Testament, Mary is presented from start to
finish as the "woman of prayer." We have just alluded to
the scene of the annunciation in Luke, chapter 1, where her
prayer is a listening to God's word as he greets her through
the angel as "full of grace" and assures her "the Lord is
with you." What ecstatic joy this word must have brought
Mary! Yet, she hears without presumption—even with a
troubled humility—that leads the angel to reassure her, "Do
not be afraid, Mary, for you have found favor with God"
(Lk 1:30).

Our prayer, too, should be above all a "listening" for
God's word to us—a word that will often bring us to a
reminder of God's personal love and care for us. Our prayer
will want also to re-echo her surrender to the inscrutable
will of God: "Behold Your servant, O God: let Your will be
done."

Fittingly, the last glimpse we have of Our Lady in the
New Testament is of her again at prayer:

> They [the apostles] went to the upper room where they
> were staying. . . . All these devoted themselves with one
> accord to prayer, together with some women, and Mary
> the mother of Jesus, and his brothers. (Acts 1:13–14)

## 3.

*"A great sign appeared in the sky, a woman clothed with the sun,*
*with the moon under her feet, and on her head a crown of twelve*
*stars." (Rev 12:1)*

This is an Advent feast. The two special readings for the
feast emphasize Mary's dignity as Mother of God. In these
days we contemplate her bearing within herself the Son of
God.

The gospel reading from Luke echoes Elizabeth's homage
to Our Lady: "Blessed are you among women, and blessed is
the fruit of your womb" (Lk 1:42). The reading from the Book
of Revelation similarly cites Mary's motherhood:

> A great sign appeared in the sky, a woman clothed with
> the sun, with the moon under her feet, and on her head
> a crown of twelve stars. She was with child and wailed
> aloud in pain as she labored to give birth. . . . She gave
> birth to a son, a male child, destined to rule all nations
> with an iron rod. (Rev 12:1–5)

The symbol of the apparition was the roses, which fell
from Juan Diego's cloak at the feet of the bishop of Mexico
City. This echoes for us the Advent prophecy of Isaiah that
God would intervene to bring salvation through a child
born of David's line: "A shoot shall sprout from the stump
of Jesse, / and from his roots a bud shall blossom. / The
Spirit of the LORD shall rest upon him: / a spirit of wisdom
and of understanding" (Is 11:1).

Christ is, of course, the bud from Jesse, and Mary is the
stem. One commentator notes:

The Advent theme is sounded: roses from a midwinter hillside signify the unexpected pure grace of Christ's coming for which we cannot really prepare and for which grace itself must make us ready.[3]

Mary's divine motherhood is pure grace. The salvation it has brought us is pure grace. On this feast may the winter roses be a joyful reminder of the supreme grace to come to us at Christmas through Mary's Son.

# $\mathcal{N}$ativity of Our Lord: Christmas

---

✣

## Historical Background

---

In many cathedrals and monasteries the ancient Christmas Martyrology is chanted on Christmas Eve, solemnly announcing this most awesome event, the appearance among us of the Son of God in human flesh taken from the Virgin Mary:

> Countless millennia after the creation of the world and the flood;

> Two thousand fifteen years after the birth of Abraham;

> One thousand five hundred ten years after Moses led the people of Israel from the land of Egypt;

One thousand thirty-two years after the anointing of David, King of Israel;

In the sixty-fifth week of the prophecy of Daniel;

In the year of the one hundred ninety-fourth Olympiad;

In the seven hundred fifty-second year after the founding of the city of Rome;

In the forty-second year of the Empire of Octavian Augustus, when the whole world was at peace;

It being the Sixth Age of the world;

Wishing to sanctify the world by his coming, nine months having elapsed since his conception by the Holy Spirit;

JESUS CHRIST, ETERNAL GOD, AND SON OF THE ETERNAL FATHER, BECAME MAN AND WAS BORN OF THE VIRGIN MARY IN BETHLEHEM OF JUDEA.

Although we do not know the actual date of Jesus' birth, the earliest liturgical observance of the coming of Our Lord appears to be on January 6 in the East, and it was more focused on the theological mystery of the manifestation of God in the flesh than on the historical details that surrounded his birth. This is still the case in many Eastern Churches.

The Church in Rome began a feast of Jesus' birth on this day, December 25, possibly to replace the pagan feast of the Unconquered Sun, or the winter solstice. As piety developed in the West much attention was given to the historical aspects of Jesus' birth as described in the gospels. This tendency came to a climax with St. Francis of Assisi's popularization of the Christmas crèche.

## Reflections

---

### I.

*"In this way the love of God was revealed to us: God sent his only Son into the world so that we might have life through him."*
*(1 Jn 4:9)*

This sentence crystallizes the mystery we celebrate on this great solemnity. It is above all else a mystery of love that should inundate our souls on this day and season. As we gaze on this visible Babe of Bethlehem "we are drawn to an immense unseen love" (Preface of Christmas). The theologian Romano Guardini wrote of this mystery:

> The Incarnation is something no human intellect can ever grasp. Indeed, it might even oppose it—yet here is the kernel of Christianity. But "love does such things"— these words come to the rescue of the mind—not that they explain anything to the intelligence; they arouse the heart, enabling it to penetrate the mystery of God. Indeed, none of the great things in human life springs from the intellect—every one issues from the heart. When it is the depth and power of God's love that stirs—is there anything of which that love is incapable?[1]

We contemplate Mother and Child on this "silent and holy night," and as we gaze at this tiny, delicate Infant held in his Mother's arms we believe and confess that here is our very God, the Infinite and Omnipotent Being who made the universe, the wonders of nature, and the complex creature that is the human person. "Though he was in the form of God . . . / he emptied himself, . . . / coming in human likeness" (Phil 2:6–7).

He makes himself present and accessible to us in a form that melts even our cold, sinful hearts. St. Ignatius in his Spiritual Exercises encourages us to take this Baby God mentally into our arms, feel the gentle stroke of his infant hand on our face, and hear the words the Prophet Isaiah speaks throughout the Advent season: "Do not be afraid, I am your Savior."

In a way, this manifestation of God as an Infant is in a form that is utterly appropriate, because the simplicity of a little child is most like the simplicity of God himself. We perhaps complicate him too much with our philosophizing and theologizing. On this day let us welcome him as he truly is: pure, simple, overflowing, gratuitous Love.

Our human, narrow, petty calculations and fears must be abandoned; the walls of our self-righteous resistance broken down; the doors of our heart thrown open to the incomprehensible immensity of God's love, which we can neither adequately fathom nor express except to repeat the inspired words of scripture: "God is love" (1 Jn 4:8). As Pope Benedict XVI wrote in his first encyclical:

> We have come to believe in God's love: in these words the Christian can express the fundamental decision of his life. Being a Christian is not the result of an ethical choice or a lofty idea, but the encounter with an event, a person, which gives life a new horizon and decisive direction.[2]

God could have brought the human family the salvation its sinful condition required in easier ways. Yet, he chose to come in Jesus and take on personally the limitations, toil, vulnerability, and sufferings of human life and then a cruel, unjust, bitter passion and death—all to prove the depth of his love for us. This is the Event and the Person that changed history and should change our lives. Realizing this we should make our own the sentiments of the Apostle Paul:

> We conquer overwhelmingly through him who loved us. For I am convinced that neither death, nor life, nor angels, nor principalities, nor present things, nor future things, nor powers, nor height, nor depth, nor any other creature will be able to separate us from the love of God in Christ Jesus our Lord. (Rom 8:37–39)

## 2.

*"I proclaim to you good news of great joy that will be for all the people. For today in the city of David a savior has been born for you who is Messiah and Lord!" (Lk 2:10–11)*

"A savior has been born!" Let us hear these words anew from the depths of our own poverty, sinfulness, and help-lessness. We have only to welcome him in humble recognition of our need; indeed, this is the message of the first beatitude: "Blessed are the poor in spirit, / for theirs is the kingdom of heaven" (Mt 5:3). If we welcome Jesus, our Savior, in this spirit there is nothing he will not lavish upon us, including the riches of his mercy, pardon, peace, healing, and love: "Come to me, all you who labor and are burdened, and I will give you rest" (Mt 11:28).

> But the question is: Does humanity of our time still await a Savior? The impression is that many think that God is foreign to their own interests. It would seem they have no need of him; they live as if he did not exist and, worse still, as if he were an "obstacle" that must be removed so they can be fulfilled. Even among believers, we are certain, some allow themselves to be drawn by seductive chimeras and distracted by deceitful doctrines which propose illusory shortcuts to attain happiness. However, despite its contradictions, anxieties, and dramas, and perhaps because of them, today's humanity seeks a way of renewal, of salvation; it seeks a Savior and awaits, sometimes unconsciously, the coming of the Lord who renews the world and our lives; the coming of Christ, the only Redeemer of man and of all men. It is true, false prophets continue to propose a "cheap" salvation which always ends by causing harsh deceptions. In fact, the history of the last fifty years shows the search for a "cheap" Savior and manifests all the disillusions that have derived from it. We Christians have the task to spread, with the testimony of life, the truth of

Christmas, which Christ brings to all men and women of
good will. Born in the poverty of the stable, Jesus comes
to offer to all the only joy and peace that can satisfy the
expectations of the human spirit.[3]

The salvation that Jesus Christ brings is incredibly rich.
He has first reconciled us sinners with his Father: "God was
reconciling the world to himself in Christ, not counting
their trespasses against them" (2 Cor 5:19). God has made
him to be our "righteousness, sanctification, and redemption" (1 Cor 1:30). There is no sin from which Jesus cannot
pardon us and free us. More than that, Jesus, the Savior,
offers us an entirely new status with God. He elevates us
from mere creatures to the dignity of adopted children of
God:

God sent his Son, born of a woman, born under the law,
to ransom those under the law, so that we might receive
adoption. (Gal 4:4–5)

One of the Christmas Antiphons speaks of the *admirabile
commercium*, the "marvelous exchange" God has made with
us: "He humbled himself to share in our humanity so that
we might be sharers in his divinity." In his Christmas sermon more than fifteen hundred years ago Pope St. Leo the
Great exclaimed: "O Christian—understand your dignity
and how you now share in God's own nature!"

"For in [Christ] dwells the whole fullness of the deity
bodily, and you share in this fullness in him" (Col 2:9–10).
This is what we mean by "living in the state of grace." Too
many Christians have an impoverished understanding of
their faith: they see it primarily as moralistic, legalistic, cer-
emonial, or ritualistic. These have a place, but the dominant
idea of Christianity is the transformation and elevation of
the human person in Jesus Christ, the new Adam. On this
Christmas we should be aware of the superabundant spiritual gifts that Christ the Savior has brought us and realize
with unlimited trust the truth of Paul's words:

He who did not spare his own Son but handed him over
for us all, how will he not also give us everything else
along with him? (Rom 8:32)

A Christian, filled with the grace of Christmas, can only
be a serene, hopeful, trusting, and joyful person!

## 3.

*"Born of the Virgin Mary, he has truly been made one of us, like
to us in all things except sin."* (Gaudium et Spes, 22)

Christmas not only draws us into the sublime supernatural
mysteries we have presented, it also casts clear light on our
daily human existence with all its challenges and even sufferings. This is true precisely because of the reality of the
Incarnation of the Son of God. Historically there has often
been a tendency to downplay the true Incarnation, the full
human reality of Jesus. In the fifth century this tendency
even reached the point of heresy in a school of thought
known as Nestorianism, which the Church condemned at
the Council of Chalcedon in AD 451.

Indeed this tendency persists today when people speak
of God's Son coming in the "disguise" of a man. Orthodox
faith holds that the Son truly and fully took on our earthly,
fleshly existence with all its limitations, emotions, needs,
and sufferings. Only sin was absent in his experience. The
Second Vatican Council proclaimed this truth anew:

He who is the "image of the invisible God" (Col 1:15), is
himself the perfect man who has restored in the children of Adam that likeness to God which had been dis-
figured ever since the first sin. Human nature, by the
very fact that it was assumed, not absorbed, in him, has
been raised in us also to a dignity beyond compare. For,
by his incarnation, he, the Son of God, has in a certain
way united himself with each man. He worked with
human hands, he thought with a human mind. He
acted with a human will, and with a human heart he

loved. Born of the Virgin Mary, he has truly been made
one of us, like to us in all things except sin. (*Gaudium et
Spes*, 22)

So we are deeply consoled that Jesus, our human brother, experienced fear, pain, disappointment, and affection.
He had to make his human journey and ministry in trust, as
do we. He was not immune to the anxieties and ambiguities
of the human condition. He is truly born today as our
brother, friend, and model for the journey of daily life. One
distinguished American theologian has expressed it well:

> The Incarnate Word does not remove the agony and the
> riddles of human existence, but takes them on himself.
> He does not abolish evil but redeems it. For the
> Christian, as for others, there will still be senseless acci-
> dents, painful illnesses, long convalescences, and cold,
> hungry days. There will be seasons of loneliness, when
> we are not welcomed or appreciated by anyone on
> earth. Death will cast its long shadow over our lives, as
> Calvary casts its shadow over Bethlehem. But, thanks to
> Christ, the promise of resurrection also casts its rays
> before it "like a lamp shining in a dark place."

> "Only in the mystery of the Incarnate Word," the recent
> Council tells us, "does the mystery of man take on
> light." Jesus enables us to believe—though not to see—
> that human life, with all its contradictions, is the place
> where God preeminently is found. Unlike every other
> mythology, the true myth of the Incarnation gives us
> strength to face up to the harsh realities of our frag-
> mented world, to feel and to transmit the touch of
> God's reconciling love. Incarnation does not provide us
> with a ladder by which to escape from the ambiguities
> of life and scale the heights of heaven. Rather, it enables
> us to burrow deep into the heart of planet earth and
> find it shimmering with divinity.[4]

## A Christmas Prayer

---

(DRAWN FROM SCRIPTURE)

Jesus—

You are the Eternal Son of the Father born in time that we might be adopted as your brothers and sisters and his children and approach him in confidence, knowing that "after such a gift He will refuse nothing";

You are the Eternal Word who has become flesh and dwelt among us, whose glory we have seen and whose fullness we have all received.

You are the Eternal Life who was with the Father from the beginning and has now become visible to us.

You are the Image of God revealing to us his humility, gentleness, patience, simplicity, and love.

You are the promised Emmanuel bearing the fullness of God's glory and essence in your body.

Jesus—I adore, glorify, praise, bless, and thank you now and for eternity.

# $\mathcal{M}$ary, Mother of God

## JANUARY 1

✤

## Historical Background

This Octave Day of Christmas brings together and celebrates a number of aspects of the Christmas mystery. The
post-conciliar liturgical reform made it a solemnity in honor
of Mary's Christmas role as the very Mother of God. That is
the chief focus of this day. As the gospel reading for this day
indicates, however, we also recall the event that occurred
on the eighth day after Jesus' birth: the Circumcision, the
first shedding of the precious blood of Christ for our salvation. Finally, the beginning of the new secular year is not
forgotten. The first reading is a solemn prayer for God's
blessing on us as we launch a new year with all its hopes
and challenges.

## Reflections

---

### I.

*"God sent his Son, born of a woman." (Gal 4:4)*

In his letter to the Galatians, one of the earliest letters of the New Testament, already Paul anticipates the Apostles' Creed in linking Mary to the Saving Incarnation. She is the privileged and essential partner of the Eternal Son in this great drama of salvation. Today, on the Octave Day of Christmas, the Church turns the spotlight on Mary, the Holy Mother who carried the Savior for nine months, gave him birth at Bethlehem, and nourished him at her breast. She is truly the *Theotokos*, the God-Bearer. With the Church all over the world today we must honor her with singular devotion: "Hers the joy of motherhood, hers the virgin's glory. Never was the like seen before, never shall it be seen again" (Antiphon in Morning Prayer).

God honors humanity by making his saving intervention dependent on the free acceptance and cooperation of a humble maiden of Nazareth. Her *fiat* was the catalyst that allowed the Eternal Son to take flesh and became both our brother and Savior. Mary's role was essential in God's plan because of the mission of the Son to be the expiating offering for the sin of humankind. St. Athanasius explains this in the reading used in today's Office:

> She is to provide him with a body of his own to be offered for our sake. . . . By taking our human nature and offering it in sacrifice, the Word was to invest it with his own (divine) nature. . . . Our Savior truly became man and from this has followed the salvation of man. (*Letter to Epictetus,* 5–9)

No wonder the daily prayer of Christians is "blessed are you among women and blessed is the fruit of your womb." She is intrinsically linked to the whole saving event. Proper acknowledgement and veneration of her is a guarantee of orthodox faith in Jesus' full mystery.

As we venerate her as true Mother of God, we also again are reminded that she is therefore also our Mother in the spiritual life. No one more than she desires that what Christ accomplished be fully effective for each of us. We can turn to her with confidence and ask for her maternal care and protection. It is this the Church prays for in the Opening Prayer of today's Mass:

> God our Father, may we always profit by the prayers of the Virgin Mother Mary, for you bring us life and salvation through Jesus Christ, her Son.

### 2.

*"When eight days were completed for his circumcision, he was named Jesus, the name given him by the angel before he was conceived in the womb." (Lk 2:21)*

Today we also note the circumcision of Jesus according to the Jewish law as mentioned in today's gospel reading. This was the first shedding of that precious blood that achieves our salvation. It is a holy moment in the mystery of Christ. Before the conciliar liturgical reform this was the focus and title of this feast day.

At the same time, as the gospel reading notes, he receives the name of "Jesus." The name refers to the Jewish general Joshua who led the Chosen People into the Holy Land. It means literally "Yahweh saves" and indicates Jesus' role and mission.

This gesture and name remind us also of Jesus' essential bond with the Jewish people. Circumcision was the sign of the first covenant. Our faith and salvation arise from that covenant and, like Jesus, we too are spiritually linked to God's Chosen People. This is a fitting day on which to pray for the coming together of Christians and Jews in ever greater faith and fidelity to the covenant. It is a fitting day

also to pray for peace in the land of Israel, asking that all
who share that holy space may learn to live together as sisters and brothers, children of one God.

## 3.

*"The Lord bless you and keep you! /*
*The Lord let his face shine upon you, and be gracious to you! / The*
*Lord look upon you kindly and give you peace!" (Nm 6:24–26)*

At the beginning of a new civil year this triple blessing of
the Lord, read from the Book of Numbers, is solemnly
invoked on us. Pope Benedict XVI gave a rich interpretation
of this New Year's prayer in his homily on January 1, 2007,
in which he also highlighted this day as the annual World
Day of Peace:

> The Lord's Name is repeated in it three times. This
> gives one an idea of the intensity and power of the
> Blessing, whose last word is "peace." The biblical term
> *shalom*, which we translate as "peace," implies that
> accumulation of good things in which consists the "sal-
> vation" brought by Christ, the Messiah announced by
> the Prophets. We Christians therefore recognize him as
> the Prince of Peace. He became a man and was born in a
> grotto in Bethlehem to bring peace to people of good
> will, to all who welcome him with faith and love. Thus,
> peace is truly the gift and commitment of Christmas:
> the gift that must be accepted with humble docility and
> constantly invoked with prayerful trust, the task that
> makes every person of good will a "channel of peace."

Thus, at the beginning of a New Year we invoke God's
blessing and his peace on ourselves, our families, and our
world. There is no better way to begin this new page in
human history and in our lives.

# $\mathcal{E}$piphany of Our Lord

## J A N U A R Y    6

✤

## Historical Background

The Greek word *epiphany* means "manifestation," in this case the manifestation of Jesus as the Incarnate Son of God, and it is this rich theological dimension of the appearing of Christ among us that the feast historically highlighted.

It is the oldest Christmas liturgical feast. It was celebrated in the East in the early second century, long before the Western Church began observing December 25. It is still the primary Christmas feast in much of the East, especially in Russia.

In this one observance three "manifestations" of Christ, the Son of God, are now included: his revelation to the Magi as described in Matthew's gospel, his revelation as God's Son at his baptism in the Jordan River, and the revelation of

his divine power at the Cana wedding feast. In the West the
first took precedence; in the East often the second. In fact, in
many Eastern Churches today water is blessed and given to
the congregation as a symbol of Jesus' baptism.

Reflections

---

I.

*"Where is the newborn king of the Jews?"*
*(Mt 2:2)*

This question of the Magi helps us focus our worship and
devotion for this great solemnity. They somehow knew and
sought a promised Messiah-King.

The prophet Malachi had long ago exclaimed: "The
Lord and Ruler is coming." These words provide the Introit
for today's Mass. The newborn Jesus is "Lord" in the most
literal sense: he shares God's divinity and, because of that,
is the true King over all the earth. His kingship was already
described in the Old Testament:

> Justice shall flower in his days,
>
> and profound peace, till the moon be no more.
>
> May he rule from sea to sea,
>
> and from the River to the ends of the earth.
>
> All kings shall pay him homage,
>
> all nations shall serve him.
>
> For he shall rescue the poor man when he cries out,
>
> and the afflicted when he has no one to help him.
>
> He shall have pity for the lowly and the poor;
>
> the lives of the poor he shall save. (Ps 72:7–8, 11–13)

This is the King the Magi sought and acknowledged in
the arms of Mary, his Mother. He is the perfect fulfillment of
the needs and desires of the human race. In the first reading

for today's Mass, the Church exultantly proclaims his manifestation among us and the effect it should have on us:

> Rise up in splendor! Your light has come,
>
> the glory of the Lord shines upon you.
>
> See, darkness covers the earth,
>
> and thick clouds cover the peoples;
>
> But upon you the Lord shines,
>
> and over you appears his glory. (Is 60:1–2)

We too are invited today to deepen our faith in Jesus as Our Lord and King, to offer him the unique adoration he deserves, and to entrust our lives to him. As has been noted before, Christianity is not a theory or an ethical system but a Person and an Event. Today's solemnity presents that Person to us in all his mystery and beauty and invites us to respond personally to the words of the Christmas hymn: "O come, let us adore him!"

Epiphany is then above all a feast of exultant joy and gratitude for this Lord-King who in the words of today's Preface has "renewed humanity in his immortal image." Christmas comes to its full plenitude on this day.

### 2.

*"We saw his star at its rising and have come to do him homage!"*
*(Mt 2:2)*

As we saw at Christmas, the Son of God crossed the boundaries of infinity and eternity to come down to us and make himself accessible to us. But we also, like the Magi, have to set out on our journey of faith to encounter him. We have to respond to "the star of faith," however it manifests itself in our lives! These ways will be many and diverse—the teaching and example of parents, the witness of a catechist, a homily that strikes us, the challenge of key events in our life.

The faith journey is the journey of a lifetime, and often it is arduous. As happened to the Magi, the star at times may become dim or even seem to disappear altogether, but we never abandon the quest; we continue with the journey of faith. The great German theologian, Fr. Karl Rahner, S.J., has poignantly captured this significant aspect of today's feast:

> This day is the feast of the blessed journey of the man who seeks God on his life's pilgrimage, the journey of the man who finds God because he seeks him. When we read of the Magi in the first twelve verses of the second chapter of Saint Matthew, we are really reading our own history, the history of our own pilgrimage. Led by the star, these Magi from far off Persia struggled through deserts and successfully asked their way through indifference and politics until they found the child and could worship him as Savior-king. It is our history that we read there.
>
> The Magi journeyed. The way was long and their feet were often tired, their hearts often heavy and vexed. And it was a strange, painful feeling for their poor hearts to have to be so entirely different from the hearts of other men, who were engrossed in their everyday affairs with such perfect stupidity, and who looked with pity at these travelers walking past on a journey that was so uselessly squandering their hearts. But their hearts carry on to the end. They do not even know where the courage and strength keep coming from. It is not from themselves, and it just suffices. When they came and knelt down, they only did what they had in reality always been doing, what they were already doing during their search and journey: they brought before the face of the invisible God now made visible the gold of their love, the incense of their reverence, and the myrrh of their suffering.[1]

# 3.

*"They all gather and come to you." (Is 60:4)*

Epiphany is more than a day of personal devotion and worship. It draws us also into the great mystery of the Church symbolized by the arrival of these mysterious gentile Magi before the newborn Lord-King. As the Second Vatican Council reminded us:

> God has willed to make men holy and save them, not as individuals without any bond or link between them, but rather to make them into a people who might acknowledge him and serve him in holiness. (*Lumen Gentium*, 9)

So in today's Mass we hear Isaiah's words: "Nations shall walk by your light. . . . / Raise your eyes and look about; / they all gather and come to you" (Is 60:3–4). Likewise, Paul proclaims that "the Gentiles are coheirs, members of the same body, and copartners in the promise in Christ Jesus through the gospel" (Eph 3:6). Today is then the "feast of the Church."

The Church, however, is more than just a people gathered from Jews and Gentiles. It is a sacrament of Christ. The saving presence of Christ, manifested on earth at Christmas and Epiphany, is continued in a real way by the Church. Through this visible and historical body Christ communicates truth and grace still in our day. So there is a direct connection between the mystery of Christmas-Epiphany and the mystery of the Church. The Second Vatican Council taught this important truth in these words:

> The society structured with hierarchical organs and the Mystical Body of Christ, the visible society and the spiritual community, the earthly Church and the Church endowed with heavenly riches, are not to be thought of as two realities. On the contrary, they form one complex reality which comes together from a human and a

divine element. For this reason the Church is compared, not without significance, to the mystery of the Incarnate Word. As the assumed nature, inseparably united to him, serves the divine Word as a living organ of salvation, so, in a somewhat similar way, does the social structure of the Church serve the Spirit of Christ who vivifies it, in the building up of the body (cf. Eph 4:15). (*Lumen Gentium*, 8)

The great English convert Cardinal Newman expressed the same truth:

The Church is a visible body, invested with or existing in invisible privileges, for the Church would cease to be the Church did the Holy Spirit leave it since its rites and forms are nourished and animated by the living power which dwells within it. Indeed, the Church is the Holy Spirit's especial dwelling-place. For while Christ came to die for us, the Spirit came to make us one in him who had died and was alive, that is, to form the Church. The Church, thus, is the Mystical Body of Christ guided by the Spirit.[2]

# Conversion of St. Paul, Apostle

⚜

## Historical Background

It appears that the earliest focus of this day's feast was the transfer of St. Paul's relics from the catacomb of St. Sebastian to the great basilica built in his honor outside the city walls of ancient Rome. In 2006 the stone coffin containing the relics of St. Paul was unearthed for the first time in centuries and exposed for public view under the high altar of the present basilica. On this day each year the pope goes to this basilica to lead solemn evening prayer.

Only in AD 717 do we first find this feast referred to as the Conversion of St. Paul in an English liturgical calendar. This focus, however, quickly dominated and become the chief object and title of the feast.

Today marks the conclusion of the eight-day Octave of Prayer for Christian Unity first promoted by Fr. Paul Wattson, an Anglican priest and convert to Catholicism, in the early decades of the twentieth century. St. Paul's constant focus on unity in the Christian community makes this a fitting coincidence: "one body and one Spirit, as you were also called to the one hope of your call; one Lord, one faith, one baptism; one God and Father of all, who is over all and through all and in all" (Eph 4:4–6). Our observance of this feast should include prayer that this truth be more fully made manifest.

## Reflections

---

## I.

*"What shall I do, sir?" (Acts 22:10)*

The first reading of today's Mass (the lectionary offers two options, Acts 22 or Acts 9) documents in dramatic fashion the moment of St. Paul's personal encounter with the risen Christ. He was struck down on the way to Damascus by the presence of Jesus, who asks, "Saul, Saul, why are you persecuting me?"

Christ calls Saul by name, reproves him for his persecution of the Christians—with whom Jesus identifies himself—and instructs Saul to "get up and go into the city and you will be told what you must do" (Acts 9:6–7).

> The central element of the whole experience is the fact of conversion. Destined to evangelize the Gentiles "to turn them from darkness to light and from the dominion of Satan to God that they may obtain the forgiveness of their sins" (Acts 26:18), Saul is called by Christ, above all, to work a radical conversion upon himself. Saul thus begins his laborious road of conversion that will last as long as he lives, beginning with unusual humility with that "what must I do, Lord?" and docilely letting

himself be led by the hand to Ananias, through whose
prophetic ministry it will be given to him to know God's
plan. (John Paul II, January 25, 1983)

The start of the conversion journey of Saul is significantly enveloped in prayer. The now humble and open Saul
gives himself up in prayer to discern and accept God's will.
Thus, Christ tells Ananias to "ask at the house of Judas for a
man from Tarsus named Saul. He is there praying" (Acts
9:11).

All of us are called to conversion, probably not in a sud-
den dramatic fashion like Saul, but still constantly day by
day we are called ever more to surrender our lives to Christ.
He calls us too by our own name with great mercy and tenderness; he calls us to abandon our special resistance to his
will and plan for our lives and to conform ourselves to that
will and plan.

If we are to respond to that call we, like Paul, must give
ourselves up to prayer, stopping the whirl of frantic activities and putting ourselves before God, saying as Paul did,
"What shall I do?" (Acts 22:10). We can all also profit in this
life-long conversion process from the guidance of a spiritual helper—our own Ananias—who can help us in our dis-
cernment of God's will. St. Paul's conversion therefore is
not just an interesting historical episode from the beginning
of the Church; rather, it is paradigmatic for our own continued journey of conversion. All of its elements apply also to
ourselves.

## 2.

*"Go into the whole world and proclaim the gospel to every
creature." (Mk 16:15)*

In God's plan, as we see dramatically today, conversion and
mission go together. When God calls, he also gives a mission. Ananias told Saul, "you will be his witness before all
to what you have seen and heard" (Acts 22:15). St. Paul's

conversion launched a tireless missionary career that took him all over the Middle East and ultimately to Rome where he was martyred under the Emperor Nero.

Today's feast then reminds us powerfully of the whole missionary dimension of the Church. The Responsorial Psalm today repeats Christ's words: "Go into the whole world and proclaim the gospel" (Mk 16:15). This was Paul's vocation but it is also the vocation of the whole Church.

We are now in the third millennium of Christianity. It is said that the first millennium involved the evangelization of Europe, the second millennium the evangelization of the Americas, and the third millennium the evangelization of Asia. There are more than a billion Chinese and almost that many Indians who do not know of God's saving love, "the good news." The Church's mission continues. In the face of this challenge, the Church can never be at rest. We know too the re-evangelization challenge in areas that were once considered Christian. A true Christian, like Paul the Apostle, will always have a wide horizon for apostolic zeal.

It is sad and unacceptable that the Catholic Church in America has lost much of its missionary fervor. In past decades thousands of priests, sisters, and laity went to all corners of the world to bring the "good news." If this is no longer the case it demonstrates a weakening of faith in God's saving plan. It is not enough for us to exist in cozy narcissistic communities simply celebrating the faith for ourselves.

> "Go into all the world and preach the Gospel to the whole creation" (Mk 16:15). Christ's command, which Paul of Tarsus welcomed with generous heart, has continued to re-echo in the Church, raising up in the course of the centuries bands of apostles ready to face hardship and toil to bring the word of salvation to the nations. The Church of today also feels the inner urge of missionary duty. She desires to serve mankind with all her powers: and the first fundamental service, essentially linked to her *raison d'etre*, is the preaching of the Gospel

to every creature. Fidelity to the Lord's missionary command requires that the Church, in her own existence, let shine through more clearly the mystery which constitutes her. (John Paul II, January 25, 1986)

## 3.

### *"Is Christ divided?" (1 Cor 1:13)*

This day marks also the closing of the Week of Prayer for Christian Unity. Paul dealt with the problem of disunity already in the primitive Church. In the face of rival factions already emerging in the community of Corinth he complained: "Is Christ divided?" (1 Cor 1:13). Paul's anguished question is still relevant today.

The divisions among Christians are one more obstacle to the universal saving mission spoken of in the prior reflection, for such divisions confuse and alienate non-believers. Hence, the Church is bound to spare no effort in its task of restoring Christian unity. We must pray for it and work for it ceaselessly.

Within the Church and within every community of the Church there must be a constant vigilance for unity and harmony. It is easy for our sinful egos to want to focus narrowly on our own special issues or agendas. We must be more concerned for the common good. All of us must hear the words of the saint we honor today, who urges us to strive "to preserve the unity of the spirit through the bond of peace" (Eph 4:3). Whatever promotes unity and harmony is from the Spirit.

It was precisely on this feast, January 25, 1959, that the newly elected and now Blessed Pope John XXIII announced in St. Paul's Basilica to startled cardinals his intention to convoke the Second Vatican Council. That council described the Catholic Church as "a sacrament or sign and instrument of intimate union with God and of the unity of the whole human race" (*Lumen Gentium*, 1). The Church then must be able to show to an ever more fractured and divided human family the way to unity. This is its mission, this was the spirit Blessed John XXIII was trying to arouse in the Church. It is needed today more than ever when we hear of "clashes of civilizations."

Prayer and efforts at Christian unity, then, cannot end with the conclusion of this week of special prayer. They must continue throughout the year and we must seize every opportunity for promoting this goal with trust in the power of God who can achieve what human beings deem impossible, "for nothing will be impossible for God" (Lk 1:37).

# $\mathcal{P}$resentation of the Lord

⚜

## Historical Background

In remembrance of the fact that the first-born children of Israel were spared the death that came upon the Egyptians at the time of the Exodus, it was prescribed in Jewish Law that every first-born should be presented to God in the Temple and then be ransomed by an offering (see Exodus 13). Forty days after Jesus' birth, Mary and Joseph accordingly brought him to the Temple for this religious ceremony.

Mary not only presented her Son to God but she herself was ritually purified as Jewish Law prescribed after childbirth. This offering of Jesus and purification of Mary become the occasion for a graced encounter of the newborn Messiah and Savior with Simeon and Anna. All these aspects are encompassed in this beautiful feast that definitively concludes the Christmas cycle.

Egeria, the Spanish nun and pilgrim, describes this feast already being observed in the fourth century in Jerusalem, along with a special procession in its honor. From there it spread into the East with the name of *Hypapante,* or "the Encounter," highlighting the meeting of Christ with Simeon and Anna. A candlelight procession acknowledging Jesus as "light of the nations," in the words of Simeon, seems to be a feature of this feast-day liturgy from very early times.

The feast caught on in Rome as a replacement for a traditional pagan procession, the Lupercalia, observed on this same day. From Rome it spread throughout the West. Before the Second Vatican Council it was primarily observed as a Marian feast, the Purification. After the council's liturgical reforms it was designated as a Christological feast, the Presentation of the Lord. Nonetheless, as in the whole Christmas cycle, it is a feast in which Mary and her Son are inextricably united.

Reflections

---

## I.

*"Sacrifice and offering you did not desire, / but a body you prepared for me." (Heb 10:5)*

The feast of the Presentation at its deepest level commemorates the consecration of the Incarnate Son, Jesus, to God the Father. The simple gesture of the presentation of this Child in the Temple by his parents contains an awesome hidden mystery that we contemplate today with the eyes of faith.

Jesus was born to give his whole being to the Father to the point of his bloody sacrifice on the cross. In a way, this feast is a bridge feast between the Christmas commemoration of his birth and the coming Holy Week when we remember his saving death. The consecration of Jesus to the Father that we note today is a prelude to his sacrificial offering of himself on the cross.

> When he came into the world, [Jesus] said:
>> "Sacrifice and offering you did not desire,
>>> but a body you prepared for me. . . .
>> 'I come to do your will, O God.'"
> . . . By this "will," we have been consecrated through the offering of the body of Jesus Christ once for all. (Heb 10:5–10)

Because of this deeper and hidden meaning of the Presentation, the Church for the reading at Mass uses the second chapter of the Letter to the Hebrews, highlighting how this Infant is indeed the Mediator between God and human beings. To carry out this role he had to assume our human nature in which he is today offered publicly to his Father:

> He had to become like his brothers in every way, that he might be a merciful and faithful high priest before God to expiate the sins of the people. (Heb 2:17–18)

His mediation for us with the Father expresses itself precisely in his solidarity with us. That is the reason for the Incarnation, which we have been celebrating since Christmas and which reaches a key moment in today's Presentation. Because he is truly God and truly man he can effect our reconciliation with God and our salvation. As we celebrate this deepest mystery of Jesus' life, we remember that we too are called to imitate and share in this offering:

> I urge you therefore, brothers, by the mercies of God, to offer your bodies as a living sacrifice, holy and pleasing to God, your spiritual worship. Do not conform yourself to this age but be transformed by the renewal of your mind, that you may discern what is the will of God, what is good and pleasing and perfect. (Rom 12:1–2)

## 2.

*"In hope we were saved." (Rom 8:24–25)*

In today's feast, Mary, Simeon, and Anna at least dimly recognize that they are entering some kind of major transition in God's dealing with his people. They do not know how it will all work out; each is content to surrender in faith to God's plan and will as it unfolds.

Mary profoundly participates in both this offering of the Infant Jesus in the Temple and his offering of himself on the cross. She is present at both, consenting in the deepest faith to God's mysterious and salvific plan being worked out through her Son. So she hears today the mysterious words of Simeon: "You yourself shall be pierced with a sword."

> The first person who is linked to Christ on the road of obedience, tested faith, and shared sorrow is his mother Mary. The Gospel text shows her in the act of offering the Son: an unconditional offering. Mary is mother of him who is "glory of his people Israel" and "light of the gentiles" but also a "sign of contradiction" (Lk 2:32–34). It is she whose immaculate soul must be pierced with a sword of sorrow to show that her role in the story of salvation is not finished in the mystery of the Incarnation, but continues in her loving and sorrowful participation in the death and resurrection of her Son. Carrying the Son to Jerusalem the Virgin Mother offers him to God as the true Lamb who will take away the sins of the world. (Pope Benedict XVI, February 2, 2006)

Since today also commemorates the rite of her purification, we can draw from that gesture an important spiritual lesson:

> The mother of all purity has seemed to be purified by the law so as to show forth, at one and the same time, the strength of all-obedient humility and the truth of the Gospel's purifying power. Where then is the man so

stubbornly and mistakenly presumptuous of his own sanctity as to refuse to undergo the cleansing action of the remedy of penance? Even if he really be holy he cannot surely be as holy as she, the most holy of all the holy, Mary who gave birth to the Holy of Holies? I only wish my dear brethren, that we, in our sinfulness, had the same humility as the saints had in their virtue.[1]

Like Mary, both Simeon and Anna have their own special roles today. Significantly, both figures are elderly. The attractions, delights, and illusions of life, so powerful in youth or middle age, no longer entice them. They have seen it all. Yet, they have one beautiful and important quality: hope!

They have reached the end of their lives with an apparently undiminished hope. Indeed, Simeon's hope remains so strong that it keeps him alive. In this Simeon and Anna are exceptional. They have not succumbed to the cynical realism that hopes for nothing. Both of them await the consolation of Israel. Experience does not teach hope: frequently it teaches the opposite. Think about what Simeon and Anna had seen in their long lifetimes: the sorrow, cruelty, selfishness, dishonesty, smallness, crime, war, and so on. Such visions do not engender hope of themselves. No, hope does not come easy. Anna and Simeon are exceptional.[2]

They are both described as "pious"; that is, they were prayerful people who kept their priorities and values in order and so were ready for the Encounter. The gospel mentions several times that they were "led by the Spirit," and so they recognized the mystery of the Child, the promised Messiah and Savior. Simeon "praises God" and Anna "speaks about the child" to others.

Like Mary, Simeon, and Anna, we too live in hope and trust, even with many unanswered questions. This often calls for true courage:

For in hope we were saved. Now hope that sees for
itself is not hope. For who hopes for what one sees? But
if we hope for what we do not see, we wait with
endurance. (Rom 8:24–25)

## 3.

*"Lead, kindly Light, amid the encircling gloom,*
*Lead thou me on."*

Today is a "feast of light." Recalling Simeon's word that
Jesus is "light to the gentiles," the Church rejoices in the
dark winter season that "her light has come." This joy is
expressed by the blessing of the candles on this day and in
the ancient tradition of the procession with lighted candles.

Jesus in John's gospel proclaims: "I am the light of the
world. Whoever follows me will not walk in darkness, but
will have the light of life" (Jn 8:12). Every disciple of Jesus
understands his or her vocation to follow the light of Christ.
John Henry Cardinal Newman expressed this poignantly in
a poem he wrote at a difficult moment of his own faith journey. It might fittingly be our prayer on this day:

Lead, kindly Light, amid the encircling gloom,
Lead thou me on;
The night is dark, and I am far from home,
Lead thou me on.
Keep thou my feet; I do not ask to see
The distant scene; one step enough for me.
I was not ever thus; nor prayed that thou
Shouldst lead me on;
I loved to choose and see my path, but now
Lead thou me on;
I loved the garish day and, spite of fears,
Pride ruled my will: remember not past years.
So long thy power hath blest me, sure it still

Will lead me on
O'er moor and fen, o'er crag and torrent, till
The night is gone,
And with the morn those Angel faces smile,
Which I have loved long since, and lost awhile.

Finally, let us remember that the light of Christ follows us from birth to death. At our baptism a lit candle is given to our godparents for us. At death a blessed candle is often lit near the dying person. The prayer for the Blessing of Candles today reminds us that we are on our way to "the light that shines forever," to that eternal dwelling place where:

Night will be no more, nor will they need light from lamp or sun, for the Lord God shall give them light, and they shall reign forever and ever. (Rev 22:5)

# $\mathcal{L}$ent

⚜

## Historical Background

Incorporation into the death and resurrection of Christ (Romans 6) by sacramental initiation is the apex of the sacred liturgy. This is especially celebrated at the Easter Vigil when Christian initiation most properly takes place, with the catechumen receiving the triple sacraments of baptism, confirmation, and eucharist. Proper participation in so awesome a mystery requires preparation of conversion and catechesis. Structurally this became known as the catechumenate and is today ritualized in the Rite of Christian Initiation of Adults (RCIA).

Lent developed as the period before Easter when a process of proximate preparation most fully unfolded. A historian of liturgy writes: "we are probably safe in seeing in this final immediate preparation of candidates for baptism the origin of that season we know as Lent."[1] Moreover, already in AD 329 a letter of St. Athanasius mentions "the fast of forty days" before Easter, and the Council of Nicaea (AD 325) likewise mentions such a practice.

At the same time many Western churches saw this period as a time for public penance by those seeking reconciliation for serious sins committed after baptism. A rite for this took place on Holy Thursday. These two streams of preparation and penance have melded in our contemporary observance of Lent. It is a time for all believers to focus on repentance and conversion and on preparation for the renewal of our baptismal vows at Easter.

Reflections

---

I.

*"If God is for us, who can be against us?" (Rom 8:31)*

The revelation of divine love that was such a focus of the Christmas season continues and intensifies in the season of Lent. Both the conversion and spiritual renewal that this season of Lent calls for are rooted in a deep awareness of the merciful love of God.

Jesus Christ Crucified reveals in the most powerful and dramatic fashion the love of God. Our lenten journey leads us ultimately to Calvary where this divine drama of sacrificial love is played out in awesome fashion. Our lenten observance then should be more Christ-focused than self-focused. It should open us up to the love of God. Whatever aids that goal is a good lenten observance; whatever distracts from it is a hindrance.

In his Message for Lent 2007, Pope Benedict XVI explained that God's love contains both elements of agape and eros. His agape is shown in his totally selfless gift of his life for our redemption. But as the pope notes, God's love contains also an element of eros—God desires our love! After noting the relevant images of the Old Testament the pope asserts:

The Almighty awaits the "yes" of His creature as a young bridegroom awaits the response of his bride. Unfortunately from the beginning humanity, seduced by the lies of Satan, closed itself to the love of God, in the illusion of an impossible autonomy. . . . To recapture the love of His creature God has consented to pay a high price: the blood of his Only begotten Son . . . on the Cross there is manifested the eros of God for us.

Lent therefore is above all a time to open ourselves to this incredible love of God. Our penances, self-denials, and acts of conversion are all ordered to free us from all that hinders our fullest acceptance of divine love. Our lenten observance should be an attempt to remove obstacles that keep us from accepting that love.

In this light we might often return in our lenten prayer to the magnificent passage of St. Paul that extols the love of God for us:

If God is for us, who can be against us? He who did not spare his own Son but handed him over for us all, how will he not also give us everything else along with him? Who will bring a charge against God's chosen ones? It is God who acquits us. Who will condemn? It is Christ [Jesus] who died, rather, was raised, who also is at the right hand of God, who indeed intercedes for us. What will separate us from the love of Christ? Will anguish, or distress, or persecution, or famine, or nakedness, or peril, or the sword? As it is written:

"For your sake we are being slain all the day;
        we are looked upon as sheep to be
        slaughtered."

No, in all these things we conquer overwhelmingly through him who loved us. For I am convinced that neither death, nor life, nor angels, nor principalities, nor present things, nor future things, nor powers, nor height, nor depth, nor any other creature will be able to

separate us from the love of God in Christ Jesus our
Lord. (Rom 8:31–39)

## 2.

*"If by the spirit you put to death the deeds of the body, you will
live." (Rom 8:13)*

Prayer, fasting, and almsgiving (various types of charity to
others) are the traditional hinges of the Church's lenten program. Each needs to have a specific part in our personal
lenten journey. These observances are especially inspired
by Jesus' forty days in the desert described in the gospels
(Mt 4:1–11; Mk 1:12–13; Lk 4:1–13) in which he fasted,
prayed, and was tempted by Satan.

Since fasting is so much a part of Lent it is useful to
reflect on what such self-denial means in the Christian context. Fasting realistically presumes that, as a result of original sin, we are inclined to misuse the good things that
surround us. We seek to find "happiness" from them by
ego-centered self-satisfaction. By fully indulging ourselves
in creature comforts we hope to find bliss here on earth.

Yet, true happiness is attained only when we are delivered from fixation upon our own self and our own satisfaction to find it in the love of God. St. John of the Cross says:
"In order to arrive at having pleasure in everything, desire
to have pleasure in nothing." Our passions and desires,
incessantly indulged, only blind, weaken, and exhaust us.

St. Paul expressed this truth:

> We are not debtors to the flesh, to live according to the
> flesh. For if you live according to the flesh, you will die,
> but if by the spirit you put to death the deeds of the
> body, you will live. (Rom 8:12–13)

Christian mortification is not a negative enterprise but a
positive one. It does not mean that the body or material
things are bad—they are not. It means that because we are
wounded and fallen sinners we tend to use these things in

an avaricious and self-absorbed way that leads us away from God instead of toward him: "The concern of the flesh is hostility toward God; it does not submit to the law of God, nor can it" (Rom 8:7). So in Lent we temper our use of food and drink so that we may subsequently enjoy them more, being more conscious of them as gifts of God and offering him praise and gratitude for them.

> True sanctity does not consist in trying to live without creatures. It consists in using the goods of life in order to do the will of God. It consists in using God's creation in such a way that everything we see and use and love gives new glory to God. To be a saint means to pass through the world gathering fruits for heaven from every tree and reaping God's glory in every field. The saint is one who is in contact with God in every possible way, in every possible direction. He is united to God in the depths of his own being. He sees and touches God in everything and everyone around him. Everywhere he goes, the world rings and resounds (though silently) with the deep harmonies of God's glory.[2]

Lenten corporeal fasting then fulfills important spiritual goals that are summarized in the lenten Mass Preface often used in this season:

> Father, you ask us to express our thanks by self-denial. We are to master our sinfulness and conquer our pride. We are to show to those in need your goodness to ourselves. (Preface III)

## 3.

*"He takes away every branch in me that does not bear fruit, and everyone that does he prunes so that it bears more fruit." (Jn 15:2)*

Discipline of the senses leads to discipline of the heart. St. John of the Cross teaches that the way to holiness leads through both the "night of the senses," which we might somewhat relate to bodily fasting, but also through the "night of the spirit." Our deepest self needs to be continually purified and, in Jesus' words, "pruned" to be able to grow in the love of God. While this process is not limited to Lent, this season seems an appropriate time to become more aware of it.

The psalms often repeat phrases like "wait upon the Lord" or "seek the Lord with all your heart." This process of "seeking" and "waiting" is part of the "night of the spirit" by which we grow closer to God. We seek him for himself and not for any consolation and security we might desire. Paradoxically, in this process God may even allow us to feel his absence, his distance—even to a painful degree. We must endure this process and not seek quick, sensible reassurances for our faith.

One writer describes this purification experience and the beautiful humility in which it results:

> God seems unreal—he is mute and silent in refusal, as if he embraces our existence only as an empty, distant horizon would embrace it; our thoughts and the demands of our heart go astray in this pathless infinity and wander around, never to find their way out. God's distance means that our spirit has become humble in the face of an insoluble puzzle. There is a distance of God that permeates the pious and the impious, that perplexes the mind and unspeakably terrifies the heart. The pious do not like to admit it because they suppose that such a thing should not happen to them (although their Lord Himself cried out, "My God, my God, why have you forsaken me?").[3]

This "night of the spirit" also means a humble recognition of our own "poverty of spirit." We might find ourselves echoing some of the sentiments of the famous pilgrim of the Russian spiritual tradition:

> Turning my eyes carefully upon myself and watching the course of my inward state, I have verified by experience that I do not love God, that I have no love for my

neighbor, that I have no religious belief, and that I am
filled with pride and sensuality.[4]

From these experiences of the "night of the senses " and
the "night of the spirit" we can more truly make our own
the words of Psalm 51, which is the Church's great lenten
prayer:

> Have mercy on me, O God, in your goodness;
>> in the greatness of your compassion wipe out my
>> offense.
> Thoroughly wash me from my guilt
>> and of my sin cleanse me.
>
> A clean heart create for me, O God,
>> and a steadfast spirit renew within me.
> Cast me not out from your presence,
>> and your holy spirit take not from me.
> Give me back the joy of your salvation
>> and a willing spirit sustain in me.
>
> I will teach transgressors your ways,
>> and sinners shall return to you.
> My sacrifice, O God, is a contrite spirit;
>> a heart contrite and humbled, O God, you will not
>> spurn. (Ps 51:3–4, 12–15, 19)

# St. Joseph, Husband of Mary

MARCH 19

## Historical Background

Joseph's role in the Saving Incarnation of the Son of God was an important one: he protected the mystery of Mary's virginity and gave Jesus legal claim to Davidic descent. His role was exercised in great humility—we have not a word from him in scripture.

Similarly the evolution of his cult in the Church was also humble and slow. There was no early feast, but the devotion to him of great saints like St. Teresa of Avila and St. Bernardine of Siena contributed to the spread of his cult, and finally by the sixteenth century there was a feast for him universally celebrated.

Reflections

---

## I.

*"It was not through the law that the promise was made to Abraham and his descendants that he would inherit the world, but through the righteousness that comes from faith." (Rom 4:13)*

Faith is the foundation of the spiritual life, and it is significant that it is this quality in St. Joseph that the Church highlights in its liturgy today. In today's gospel reading, Joseph obediently hears the word of God, and without questioning or equivocating he responds totally. The second reading today from Romans speaks of the "righteousness that comes from faith." But Joseph was not a theologian or a mystic; he was a "simple believer." In this context we can appreciate the words of Pope Benedict XVI:

> The simple faith of simple souls merits the respect, the reverence of the preacher, who has no right simply to pit his intellectual superiority against a faith which has remained simple and which, by its simple and intuitive comprehension of the Faith as a whole, can in some cases understand the essence of that Faith more profoundly than is possible for a reflective faith that is fragmented by division into systems and theories. In my view, what is fundamental here is the insight that the transition from the Old to the New Testament actually took place in the faith of simple souls: it was the *anawin* ("the poor") who associated themselves neither with the liberalism of the Sadducees nor with the literal orthodoxy of the Pharisees. Because of their simple intuitive comprehension of the Faith, their lives were based on an absolute confidence in its promise and precepts and so became the locale in which the Old Testament could be transformed into the New Testament: Zechariah, Elizabeth, Mary, Joseph, Jesus

himself. The "faith of the poor" continues to be the most precious treasure of the Church.[1]

## 2.

*"He went and dwelt in a town called Nazareth." (Mt 2:23)*

A second aspect of Joseph's holiness that is relevant for all of us is that it was achieved in the ordinariness of daily life. While today we rightly honor Joseph as one of the greatest saints of all time, we need to remember that his life was filled with silence, humility, and faithfulness to ordinary activities. As a man of faith he filled these ordinary activities with the love of God. It was in the faithful carrying out of the daily duties of father, husband, and carpenter that he fulfilled God's will and achieved his sanctity.

Some approaches to sanctity seem to so emphasize the extraordinary—even the esoteric—that they place holiness out of the reach of ordinary mortals. Joseph is a reminder that we find God and holiness in the fabric of our daily, normal lives, our duties, family relationships, and the ordinary trials and sufferings of daily life. This is the normal road to sanctity. Joseph's way of holiness was in the basic virtues that transform daily life: faith, love of God, trust in God's plan and purpose no matter what comes, humility, and self-sacrificing love for others—as he sacrificed himself for Mary and Jesus.

## 3.

*"Joseph rose and took the child and his mother by night and departed for Egypt." (Mt 2:14)*

While Joseph's path to sanctity was quiet and humble, it was by no means easy. Joseph had to constantly adjust as he responded to God's will. He was betrothed to Mary before her virginal conception of Jesus. Then, after learning of her conception, he adjusted to a new way of relating to Mary and a new understanding of their marriage. He undertook the journey to Bethlehem when Caesar ordered a census. He rescued Mary and Jesus from the plots of Herod and took them to Egypt, with all the difficulties such a journey involved. Finally, he had to adjust to the mystery of this boy whom God had entrusted to his fatherly care even though, as the gospels tell us, Mary and Joseph could not fully understand him or the divine plan into which they had been drawn.

May the example and prayer of St. Joseph help us to find God's will in the basic and ordinary realities of daily life just as he did—living from moment to moment in total trust and surrender to the loving God who guides our lives.

# $\mathcal{A}$nnunciation of the Lord

## MARCH 25

❧

## Historical Background

Nine months prior to the celebration of the birth of the Lord, the Church observes the Solemnity of the Annunciation to Mary by the angel Gabriel. Mary's free consent made possible the virginal conception of the Eternal Son of God as her son. This feast was common in the East by AD 650 and soon thereafter was adapted also in the West. If it occurs in Holy Week it is transferred to the Monday after the second Sunday of Easter.

Prior to the Second Vatican Council's reform of the liturgy, this day was considered primarily a Marian feast, but the post-conciliar reform established it as a feast of the Lord. As with the feast of the Presentation on February 2, however, there is an intimate connection between the

Lord's Incarnation and the essential role of his mother, and so both are the object of our prayer on this feast.

## Reflections

---

### I.

*"He emptied himself, / taking the form of a slave." (Phil 2:7)*

On this feast of the Lord a dominant sentiment is one of profound adoration before the mystery of God taking human flesh. The Church expresses this today by asking us to kneel when we pray in the Creed: "he came down from heaven: by the power of the Holy Spirit he was born of the Virgin Mary and became man." This special gesture of worship recognizes the awesome nature of the mystery we celebrate.

The Divine Son, who from eternity had existed in the bosom of the Father and had been his instrument in the creation of the universe, now "empties himself" of his glory and "takes the form of a slave." The human mind will never be able to comprehend this union of divinity and humanity, majesty and lowliness, transcendence and immanence. Yet, it is the core of our Christian faith and the cause of our salvation.

One writer expresses well the ultimate reason for the mystery we adore and celebrate today:

> There could be nothing lacking in the bosom of the Father. God were not God, if He fell short of self-sufficiency. Yet deep in His unfathomable wisdom there was something which looks to our eyes like a want . . . it is as if God could not contain Himself, as if he were overcharged with the fullness of His own essence and beauty. . . it seems that He must go out of Himself and summon creatures up from nothing and then fall upon their neck and overwhelm them with His love. . . . Alas—how words tremble and go wild when they venture to treat the things of God! **God's love must outflow.** It seems like a necessity.[1]

## 2.

*"For our sake he made him to be sin who did not know sin, so that we might become the righteousness of God in him." (2 Cor 5:21)*

The Incarnation not only helps us discover the mystery of the unfathomable love of God but it also helps us discover our own dignity and worth. As the Second Vatican Council alerted us:

> It is only in the mystery of the Word made flesh that the mystery of man truly becomes clear. . . . Christ the Lord, Christ the new Adam, in the very revelation of the mystery of the Father and of his love, fully reveals man to himself and brings to light his most high calling. (*Gaudium et Spes*, 22)

One Cistercian monk has expressed this dimension of the mystery well:

> The event of the Incarnation of Our Lord makes us forever look at our own humanity in a completely new light. Now, in the Incarnate Word, God and humanity are united; we remain distinct, yes, but now forever inseparable. . . . Even more astounding and significant, as St. Paul tells the Corinthians: "For our sake, he (the Incarnate Son of God) was made to be sin who did not know sin, so that we might become the righteousness of God in him" (2 Cor 5:21). Thus, the very purpose of the Incarnation is to establish full communion between God and humanity, so that in Christ we may find adoption and immortality, often called "deification" by the Fathers of the Church. It is hard for us to imagine how much we, in our humanity, have been affected by the Incarnation.[2]

The impact of the Incarnation for our lives was expressed one thousand years earlier by another Cistercian monk and abbot:

The good news of our salvation was announced to
Mary today . . . that utterance, while it promises the
Virgin a Son, promises the guilty forgiveness, prisoners
redemption, captives liberty, and the buried life. That
word, while it proclaims to Mary the kingdom of the
Son, announces also the glory of the just, strikes fear
into hell and gladdens the heavens. . . . Who then is not
gladdened by that word? Who is not consoled? "Be
mindful," says King David, "of your word to your servant which gave me hope. For this has consoled me in
my humiliation." He had received only the word of
promise . . . what a joy, what a delight should the fulfillment be for us! Let us bestir ourselves with some devotion to give glory to the grace of God and to welcome
with joy the word of our salvation.[3]

## 3.

*"Hail, favored one!" (Lk 1:28)*

We cannot leave this great feast without also contemplating
the essential role of Mary, to whom this annunciation was
made. She is the privileged instrument through whom the
Saving Incarnation took place.

The words of reverence and greeting to her in today's
gospel are truly extraordinary: "Hail, favored one! The
Lord is with you. . . . You have found favor with God" (Lk
1:28-30). Already in the second century Origen noted that
nowhere else in the scriptures are such words addressed to
a human being!

Mary of Nazareth is drawn into the most awesome saving plan of God as a necessary and indispensable partner.
Pope Paul VI coined the phrase *Alma socia Redemptoris*,
"most loving helper of the Redeemer." We can only specu-
late on the impact this annunciation had on the young
virgin of Nazareth, but the Gospel gives a hint—"she was
greatly troubled"—and the angel had to reassure her, "Do
not be afraid, Mary" (Lk 1:29-30). As always, God chooses

the lowliest and most unlikely as the special instrument of his purposes.

St. Bernard of Clairvaux dramatizes this scene in eloquent language:

> You have heard, O Virgin, that you will conceive and bear a son; you have heard that it will not be by man but by the Holy Spirit. The angel awaits an answer; it is time for him to return to God who sent him. We too are waiting, O Lady, for your word of compassion; the sentence of condemnation weighs heavily upon us. The price of our salvation is offered to you. We shall be set free at once if you consent. In the eternal Word of God we all came to be, and behold, we die. In your brief response we are to be remade in order to be recalled to life.
>
> Tearful Adam with his sorrowing family begs this of you, O loving Virgin, in their exile from Paradise. Abraham begs it, David begs it. All the other holy patriarchs, your ancestors, ask it of you, as they dwell in the country of the shadow of death. This is what the whole earth waits for, prostrate at your feet. It is right in doing so, for on your word depends comfort for the wretched, ransom for the captive, freedom for the condemned, indeed, salvation for all the sons of Adam, the whole of your race.
>
> Answer quickly, O Virgin. Reply in haste to the angel, or rather through the angel to the Lord. Answer with a word, receive the Word of God. Speak your own word, conceive the divine Word. Breathe a passing word, embrace the eternal Word. Why do you delay, why are you afraid?
>
> Believe, give praise, and receive. Let humility be bold, let modesty be confident. This is no time for virginal simplicity to forget prudence. In this matter alone, O prudent Virgin, do not fear to be presumptuous. Though modest silence is pleasing, dutiful speech is

now more necessary. Open your heart to faith, O blessed Virgin, your lips to praise, your womb to the Creator. See, the desired of all nations is at your door, knocking to enter. If he should pass by because of your delay, in sorrow you would begin to seek him afresh, the One whom your soul loves. Arise, hasten, open. Arise in faith, hasten in devotion, open in praise and thanksgiving. *Behold, the handmaid of the Lord,* she says, *be it done to me according to your word.*[4]

As today we hear Mary's *fiat*—"let it be"—let us turn to her and ask that she enfold us in her maternal care that we too may echo that simple but essential prayer as we, like her, respond to God's call at each moment in the journey of our lives.

# $\mathcal{S}$unday of the Lord's Passion:
# Palm Sunday

✤

## Historical Background

The pilgrim nun Egeria describes Palm Sunday in Jerusalem in AD 383. She narrates for us a procession from the Mount of Olives, down the hill, across the valley, and into the gates of Jerusalem. This journey imitates the procession of Jesus and his followers, as described especially in John's gospel, on the day after his stay in Bethany, six days before Passover (Jn 12:1–36). This same ritual is followed today in Jerusalem when on this day the Catholic Latin patriarch marches on the same route with his faithful and many pilgrims from all over the world.

The post-conciliar liturgical reform has made this procession a triumphant celebration of the paschal victory of Jesus. The Church's ministers are vested in bright red vestments of victory, and the hymns hail Christ as Victor-King: "All glory, laud, and honor to you, Redeemer King." Liturgy, however, is never just a reenactment of past historical events. Rather, in a mysterious way it makes those events present and efficacious for us. On Palm Sunday, Christ renews the power of that first Holy Week; he comes to the new Jerusalem, the Church, to make present anew his saving work. It begins a week of exceptional grace.

Reflections

---

### I.

*"He proceeded on his journey up to Jerusalem." (Lk 19:28)*

As Pope John Paul II expressed it, every year on this special Sunday, "the curtain rises once again on the definitive drama of all history—the drama of man's redemption." As we contemplate these events of the first Palm Sunday from the historical point of view we might wonder what was in the heart and mind of the Lord Jesus on that Sunday. Perhaps one writer has a good insight into that question. He bases his insight on his contemplation of a fourteenth-century sculpture in the Augustiner Museum in Freiburg entitled "Christ on a Donkey":

> As he rides into Jerusalem surrounded by people shouting "hosanna," "cutting branches from the trees and spreading them in his path" (Mt 21:8), Jesus appears completely concentrated on something else. He does not look at the excited crowd. He does not wave. He sees beyond all the noise and movement to what is ahead of him: an agonizing journey of betrayal, torture, crucifixion, and death. His unfocused eyes see what nobody around him can see; his high forehead reflects a knowledge of things to come far beyond anyone's understanding.
>
> There is melancholy, but also peaceful acceptance. There is insight into the fickleness of the human heart,

but also immense compassion. There is a deep awareness of the unspeakable pain to be suffered, but also a strong determination to do God's will. Above all, there is love, an endless, deep, and far-reaching love born from an unbreakable intimacy with God and reaching out to all.[1]

## 2.

*"When he entered Jerusalem the whole city was shaken."*
*(Mt 21:10)*

Turning from Jesus to his disciples and the crowd on that day, we know it was a very important event in the ministry of Jesus. According to John (12:12–36) it occurred around the Passover when a great crowd of pilgrims were in Jerusalem for the feast. Many had heard of Jesus and his miracles and were anxious to see him. There was excitement and fervor among the crowd. Jesus mounts a lowly donkey, wishing to fulfill the prophecy of Zechariah: "Your king comes to you, / meek and riding on an ass, / and on a colt, the foal of a beast of burden" (Mt 21:5). The enthusiasm of the crowd grows and they wave palm branches and break into exclamations: "Blessed is he who comes in the name of the Lord"; "Hosanna to the Son of David" (the Messiah/King).

> What was the meaning of the welcome given to Jesus by the people of Jerusalem and the people who had come to the city from all over the country? It had a very special meaning, that of recognizing Jesus as Messiah.

> What was the meaning at that time of the title of Messiah? The Messiah meant someone invested with the dignity of priesthood and kingship, one in whom were realized the hopes of the Hebrews, the one who was to present the perfect figure of the ideal King, bringing liberation from foreign domination and affirmation

of the glory and surpassing destiny that by a mysterious design were to be Israel's lot (cf. Jn 1:41; 4:25).

The title had as yet no precise meaning, but in Jesus' time it dominated imaginations and minds that were restive and confident that the Messiah's time had come (cf. Mt 24:23). It was the title that expressed the eschatological, that is to say, the final hope of Israel, for the Chosen People. The episode of the palms therefore marks a decisive moment in the Gospel, a moment of extraordinary importance: Jesus is recognized, is proclaimed as the Messiah; he is acclaimed as the Christ.[2]

Our participation in the liturgical procession of palms two thousand years later, our clutching and taking home a piece of blessed palm, participates in this meaning. It is an act of faith in Christ by us, a demonstration that we too accept Jesus as the Messiah, the Savior, the Christ, sent by God the Father in his name to bring the good news of salvation to the human family and to establish the true kingdom that transcends all nations and peoples—a kingdom of truth, justice, grace, love, and peace. We acknowledge today that Jesus of Nazareth is the center of human history, the arbiter of its fate, and the personal Lord of our lives.

## 3.

*"Whoever wishes to come after me must deny himself, take up his cross, and follow me." (Mk 8:34)*

The notion of Jesus as the Messiah, however, created a problem for the Jews of that time as it does for many in our day as well. The crowd waved palm branches—signs of power and victory. The Messiah that many were expecting was a warrior king who would overthrow the Roman conquerors and restore Israel to the political greatness and status it had known in the peak years of its history under King David and King Solomon.

Instead, however, of a worldly powerful king, they were presented with a Messiah who chose to identify himself as a "servant," who washed the feet of his disciples, who went about healing the most wretched and despised and giving hope to the ostracized. The crowd's ideas and expectations of how God would act in history were shattered. We know how difficult this was even for the closest disciples who heard Jesus speak daily:

> He began to teach them that the Son of Man must suffer greatly, and be rejected by the elders, the chief priests, and the scribes, and be killed, and rise after three days. He spoke this openly. Then Peter took him aside and began to rebuke him. At this he turned around and, looking at disciples, rebuked Peter and said, "Get behind me, Satan. You are thinking not as God does, but as human beings do."

> He summoned the crowd with his disciples and said to them, "Whoever wishes to come after me must deny himself, take up his cross, and follow me. For whoever wishes to save his life will lose it, but whoever loses his life for my sake and that of the gospel will save it. What profit is there for one to gain the whole world and forfeit his life?"(Mk 8:31–36)

It is fitting then that this Sunday is liturgically entitled the "Sunday of the Lord's Passion" and features the solemn proclamation of the passion and death of Jesus. This narration shows us the true nature of Jesus' kingship and the implications of our following him. It is a message many in our modern world do not wish to hear:

> There was a time—and it has not yet been completely surmounted—in which Christianity was rejected precisely because of the Cross. The Cross speaks of sacrifice it was said, the Cross is the sign of the denial of life. Instead, we want to live in its entirety, without restrictions and without sacrifices. We want to live life, all we want is to live.

Let us not allow ourselves to be limited by precepts and prohibitions; we want richness and fullness—this is what was said and is still being said. All this sounds convincing and seductive; it is the language of the serpent that says to us: "Do not be afraid! Quietly eat the fruit of all the trees in the garden!"

Palm Sunday, however, tells us that the great "Yes" is precisely to the Cross; that the Cross is itself the true tree of life. We do not find life by possessing it, but by giving it. Love is a gift of oneself, and for this reason it is a way of true life symbolized by the Cross.[3]

The "following of Christ" then means taking the road of humility, sacrifice, selfless love of others, even suffering as God may ordain—this is the "royal road of the cross," which Jesus' followers are invited to walk. It is the liberating road of true happiness in which one finds oneself by losing oneself. One twentieth-century Church leader who walked this road by courageous fidelity to Christ's teaching unto death shared this vision with his flock:

Holy Week is a call to follow Christ's austerities, the only legitimate violence, the violence that he does to himself and that he invites us to do to ourselves: "Let those who would follow me deny themselves," be violent to themselves, repress in themselves the outbursts of pride, kill in their heart the outbursts of greed, of avarice, of conceit, of arrogance. Let them kill it in their heart. This is what must be killed, this is the violence that must be done, so that out of it a new person may arise, the only one who can build a new civilization: a civilization of love.[4]

# $\mathcal{E}$aster

✣

## Historical Background

About 1200 years before Christ, the enslaved Israelites were liberated by God from their servitude in Egypt. In one fateful night, while the Lord slew every first-born Egyptian, the Israelites were spared through the sign of the blood of the sacrificed lamb on their doorposts. They then fled Egypt and were led by Moses through the Red Sea, taking only unleavened bread with them. God made a covenant with the Israelites and thus they become his own people. All of this was memorialized in the feast of the Pasch, the Passover, which became the primary Jewish cultic celebration of the year. Before his passion, Jesus himself celebrated the Passover with his disciples.

"Our paschal lamb, Christ, has been sacrificed. Therefore, let us celebrate the feast, not with the old yeast, the yeast of malice and wickedness, but with the unleavened bread of sincerity and truth" (1 Cor 5:7–8). With these words St. Paul explains to one of the first Christian communities that the death and resurrection of Christ is the new Passover, the event of our salvation in his precious blood. It is therefore the central feast of the Christian Church. Moreover, we see that a continuity of the Jewish and Christian Passover is established, reflecting the truth that God has one saving plan for the whole human family, which began with Moses and the Jewish Exodus and culminated with Jesus Christ and his passing from death to life.

A Greek text, the Letters of the Apostles, dating from the second half of the second century, in Asia Minor, already speaks of an Easter night vigil of prayer ending with an "agape," which must be understood to include the eucharist.[1] From the Christian writer Tertullian, at the beginning of the third century, we learn that in North Africa baptism was included in the Easter celebration—a practice that expressed well the theology of baptism that Paul developed in chapter 6 of his letter to the Romans. The other Easter liturgical observances developed over many centuries, and elements from different places were ultimately integrated into the Easter night and Easter day liturgies as we know them today.

## Reflections

---

### I.

*"For I handed on to you as of first importance what I also received: that Christ died for our sins in accordance with the scriptures; that he was buried; that he was raised on the third day in accordance with the scriptures; that he appeared to Kephas, then to the Twelve." (1 Cor 15:3–5)*

In this first written account we possess of the resurrection, Paul passes it on soberly as a doctrine that he has received from the apostolic Church of Jerusalem. The narrations of the resurrection in the gospels, however, are extraordinarily

vivid and dynamic and ring true with the confusion, unbe-
lief, and only gradual acceptance described.[2] We see Peter
and John literally racing to the empty tomb, the Eleven baf-
fled and annoyed that the first announcement was brought
by women, attempts to bribe guards, and the gloom of the
sad disciples on the way to Emmaus.

The core reality, however, is at once a historical fact and
a dogma of faith: the crucified and buried Jesus was raised
to a new and transfigured corporeal existence. It is very
important to stress this fact in our moment of history when
there is a widespread tendency to relegate the "religious" to
a realm of mere inwardness and therefore only personal
and subjective meaning. The central Christian dogma and
the great feast that celebrates it are about something exter-
nal and factual that God has done. Over and over in the
liturgy of these days we repeat the words of Psalm 118:

> "The right hand of the Lord has struck with power:
>
> the right hand of the Lord is exalted."
>
> I shall not die, but live,
>
> and declare the works of the Lord.
>
> The stone which the builders rejected
>
> has become the cornerstone.
>
> By the Lord has this been done;
>
> it is wonderful in our eyes. (Ps 118:15–16a, 17, 22–23)

In the face of the modern prejudice that anything "religious" or "spiritual" is merely a matter of sentiment or
emotion it is helpful to hear these words from a modern
Catholic theologian:

> Easter tells us that God had done something. God
> himself . . . God has raised his Son from the dead, God
> has quickened the flesh. God has conquered death. He
> has done this—he has conquered—not merely in the
> realm of inwardness, in the realm of thought, but in
> the realm where we, the glory of the human mind
> notwithstanding, are most really ourselves: in the

actuality of this world, far from all "mere" thoughts and "mere" sentiments. He has conquered in the realm where we experience practically what we are in essence: children of the earth, who die.[3]

At Easter, therefore, above all we glorify, praise, and thank the Father for what he has done in and for Jesus Christ on this day in truly raising his human body from death. But we also remember: "Christ has been raised from the dead, the firstfruits of those who have fallen asleep. For since death came through a human being, the resurrection of the dead came also through a human being. For just as in Adam all die, so too in Christ shall all be brought to life" (1 Cor 15:20–22). What has happened to Christ is also our destiny. His resurrection is a guarantee and pledge that the Father will do the same for us one day. In Jesus' time one major segment of Jews, the Sadducees, did not believe in the general resurrection. Jesus explicitly and clearly opposed them by insisting on this truth (see Mk 12:18–27).

So on this Easter day our Christian faith triumphs over the shifting, changing, and undependable barometer of our personal moods and feelings to rejoice in the power and faithfulness of God to whom we entrust our human destiny. He has acted on Jesus and he will act on us.

2.

*Think of what is above, not of what is on earth. For you have died, and your life is hidden with Christ in God." (Col 3:2–3)*

Despite the objectivity and factualness of our Easter faith it is vital to realize that this is not an abstract faith or just a theological doctrine, a proposition to which we give notional intellectual assent and then move on to ordinary human life.

The resurrection is a mystery in which we are deeply involved and immersed. It is the inner source of our Christian life and holiness. With Christ we die, are buried, and rise to a new life. This is radically effected for us in baptism and renewed by every eucharist. There is no such thing, therefore, as detached faith—Christ's risen life must inundate us, transform us, elevate, and divinize us. It completely changes our human existence—even if we cannot now adequately grasp, understand, or experience it. This is what one of the readings for Easter Mass reminds us:

> If then you were raised with Christ, seek what is above, where Christ is seated at the right hand of God. Think of what is above, not of what is on earth. For you have died, and your life is hidden with Christ in God. When Christ your life appears, then you too will appear with him in glory. (Col 3:1–4)

John's gospel powerfully reminds us of this new life of Christ into which we have been inserted. Jesus says to his disciples:

> I am the vine, you are the branches. Whoever remains in me and I in him will bear much fruit, because without me you can do nothing. . . . If you remain in me and my words remain in you, ask for whatever you want and it will be done for you. By this is my Father glorified, that you bear much fruit and become my disciples. As the Father loves me, so I also love you. Remain in my love. (Jn 15:5–9)

Authentic Christian spirituality flows from an intimate and true union of life and love with Jesus Christ that grows and develops over a lifetime—"bearing fruit" in our daily life and shedding its radiance on our works and on our relationships. A Christocentric spirituality is based on the realization that Jesus is "the way and the truth and the life" (Jn 14:6). He is present to us at every moment. In our sufferings and struggles he is present, allowing us to share in his Paschal Mystery: "I have been crucified with Christ; yet I live, no longer I, but Christ lives in me" (Gal 2:19–20). The heart of this spirituality is an intimate personal relationship with Jesus Christ—especially expressed through prayer.

## 3.

*"Blessed be the God and Father of our Lord Jesus Christ, who in his great mercy gave us a new birth to a living hope through the resurrection of Jesus Christ from the dead." (1 Pt 1:3)*

A major fruit of our celebration of what God has done at Easter must be a great increase of Spirit-inspired hope and joy in us. An Easter Christian is not a person overcome by sadness, pessimism, or fear. We have been born anew "to a living hope through the resurrection of Jesus Christ!"

> Easter is a serene and deep invitation to joy. It is the joy of Christ's definitive victory over sin and death, the joy of the reconciliation of the world with the Father and the unity of mankind, the joy of new creation by the Spirit. . . . The sign of a true Christian existence is joy. It is also the best testimony of authenticity in consecrated life. . . . The best witness of the early Christian community—united in the Word, the Eucharist, and Service—was "glad and generous hearts" (Acts 2:46). Today it is necessary to recover paschal joy. For the worst sign of the disintegration of a community is sadness and fear. Jesus asks us again: "Why are you afraid? Have you no faith?" (Mk 4:40)[4]

The world around us and perhaps our own lives are filled with intractable and seemingly irresolvable problems and challenges. Yet it is precisely this that should evoke our Easter faith, hope, and joy. The risen Jesus allows us to discover the true face of God, a God-Man whose risen body bears the scars of bodily wounds he received as a result of the sinful hate and cruelty of human beings. Pope Benedict XVI in his Easter Message of 2007 makes the bold statement: "Only a God who loves us to the extent of taking upon himself our wounds and pain, especially innocent suffering, is worthy of faith."

Easter joy and hope do not fear or shrink from pain, suffering, and conflict. We know that they are ultimately vanquished in Christ. Easter faith gives us the courage to confront the hate, selfishness, violence, and suffering of this world and be apostles of reconciliation, love, peace, and joy.

# 𝒜scension of the Lord

✤

## Historical Background

According to the Acts of the Apostles, Jesus appeared to his disciples over the course of forty days (Acts 1:3) and then "was lifted up, and a cloud took him from their sight" (Acts 1:9). One theologian has pointed out the double significance of this mystery:

First, the entrance of Jesus' glorified humanity into the Trinitarian communion with the Father and Spirit: "The ascension is not a spatial voyage nor a mythical event without an objective and true reality—the 'heaven' of the ascension is the very life of the Trinitarian communion."[1]

Second, Jesus' presence to his community, the Church, in a new way: now no longer limited to the spatial-temporal confines of Palestine. Of his new form of existence he says: "I am with you always, until the end of the age" (Mt 28:20). "The ascension is not a loss of Jesus in the immensity of heaven but his more full immersion in the community of his disciples on whom he pours the grace of his divine love."[2]

## Reflections

---

### I.

*"Father . . . I glorified you on earth by accomplishing the work
that you gave me to do. Now glorify me, Father, with you, with
the glory that I had with you before the world began."*
(Jn 17:1, 4–5)

Jesus has now completed his earthly mission: love's
redeeming work is done. This feast brings to a climax and
conclusion his whole human presence among us: "I . . .
have come into the world. Now I am leaving the world and
going back to the Father" (Jn 16:28).

Jesus, the Son of God, shared with us all that was human,
except sin. He grew, he worked, he ate, he slept, he loved his
friends, he wept, he was sensitive to the natural world and to
the people around him. In all of this he has transformed our
human life and given it a value and meaning it would never
have had without his Incarnation. More than that, he gener-
ously fulfilled the mission given him by the Father: "Father . . .
I revealed your name to those whom you gave me"
(Jn 17:6). As one theologian has expressed it:

> He gave a name to the incomprehensible puzzle behind
> all things. He called it "Father" and he invited us too to
> whisper into the divine darkness "Our Father."[3]

Finally, he gave us all that he had: "This is my body that
is for you" (1 Cor 11:24). There was nothing more to do! The
cross and the eucharist were his ultimate legacy of love. His
mission was complete!

For forty days after his resurrection he appeared to and
reassured the disciples who had failed him in his hour of
need that he understood, loved, and forgave them and still
wanted them to share his great enterprise of bringing the
kingdom of God to earth. Now he comes to this last visible

moment with his community of disciples. His last greeting includes the prophetic promise of the Holy Spirit: "You will receive power when the holy Spirit comes upon you, and you will be my witnesses" (Acts 1:8). Then Jesus rises up, leaves the earth, and disappears; he hides himself. Pope Paul VI expressed the result in these striking words: "Our eyes will burn with the untiring desire to see him" (Ascension homily, 1975). We live on his memory, we wait for his return, but Jesus remains now to us invisible.

> Christ's ascension means that he no longer belongs to the world of corruption and death that conditions our life. It means that he belongs entirely to God. He, the Eternal Son, led our human existence into God's presence, taking with him flesh and blood in a transfigured form.[4]

## 2.

*"Father . . . I made known to them your name and I will make it known, that the love with which you loved me may be in them and I in them." (Jn 17:25, 26)*

Jesus disappears but he is not absent! Now to the eyes of faith a whole new vista of his ongoing saving work opens up for the believer. In fact, as St. Leo the Great puts it, "He now began to be indescribably more present in his divinity to those whom he was removed in his humanity."

The scriptures are rich with their description of the activity of the ascended Lord. Two books of the New Testament especially reveal this eternal transcendent ministry: in John's gospel, Jesus prays eternally and efficaciously for us:

> I pray for them. . . . Holy Father, keep them in your name. . . . keep them from the evil one. . . . Consecrate them in the truth. . . .

> I have given them the glory you gave me. . . . I wish that
> where I am they may also be with me, that they may see
> my glory that you gave me. . . . I made known to them
> your name and I will make it known, that the love with
> which you loved me may be in them and I in them.
> (Jn 17:9–26)

All our confidence lies in this ceaseless intercession of
the Divine Son for us. He is now our Advocate with the
Father. His greatest desire is to share with us his glory and
his love, to have us one with him and with his Father. The
book of Hebrews also presents the ascended Jesus as the
eternal compassionate high priest and victim for us:

> We have a great high priest who has passed through the
> heavens, Jesus, the Son of God. . . . For we do not have a
> high priest who is unable to sympathize with our weak-
> nesses, but one who has similarly been tested in every
> way, yet without sin. So let us confidently approach the
> throne of grace to receive mercy and to find grace for
> timely help. (Heb 4:14)

The ascended Lord's work is not restricted to us as individuals but also includes his active direction of the Church,
his body. He unites us all mysteriously to himself, sharing
his divine life and grace with the whole Mystical Body:

> In one Spirit we were all baptized into one body . . . and
> we were all given to drink of one Spirit. . . .
> Now you are Christ's body, and individually parts of it.
> (1 Cor 12:13, 27)

The Letter to the Ephesians narrates how the ascended
Christ directly bestows the offices, ministries, and charisms
on his Church:

> But grace was given to each of us according to the
> measure of Christ's gift. Therefore, it says:
>
> "He ascended on high and took prisoners captive;
> he gave gifts to men."

What does "he ascended" mean except that he also descended into the lower [regions] of the earth? The one who descended is also the one who ascended far above all the heavens, that he might fill all things.

And he gave some as apostles, others as prophets, others as evangelists, others as pastors and teachers, to equip the holy ones for the work of ministry, for building up the body of Christ. (Eph 4:7–12)

## 3.

*"Men of Galilee, why are you standing there looking at the sky?"*
*(Acts 1:11)*

Finally, the Ascension is the feast of the Church's mission. A new era now begins—the Church must pick up the mission of Christ in the world. It will be empowered to do this in a few days by the coming of the Holy Spirit on Pentecost.

The ascension is the connecting point between the mission of Jesus and that of the Church. His work is not yet complete. Can we not sense this in the question of the angels to the disciples: "Men of Galilee, why are you standing there looking up at the sky?" (Acts 1:11). There is work to be done, a world to be evangelized. "You are to be my witnesses!" is Jesus' final command. The disciples' mission will be to proclaim him as the Saving Lord (Acts 18). By the sacraments they will bring believers into living contact with him.

A recent survey indicates that in the United States the percentage of people who call themselves Christian has dropped by 11 percent in a generation and that the number who claim no religion at all has greatly risen (American Religious Identification Survey). Many factors undoubtedly contribute to this sad phenomenon—upward mobility, lack of roots, secularism, poor catechesis.

Catholics are challenged more than ever to be willing to explain and defend their faith, participate in evangelization efforts, and pray that the "good news" be effectively spread and heard.

## Novena for Pentecost

As we read in the Acts of the Apostles:

> When they entered the city they went to the upper room where they were staying, Peter and John and James and Andrew, Philip and Thomas, Bartholomew and Matthew, James son of Alphaeus, Simon the Zealot, and Judas son of James. All these devoted themselves with one accord to prayer, together with some women, and Mary the mother of Jesus, and his brothers. (Acts 1:13–14)

This is the first novena in the history of the Church—the nine days between Ascension and Pentecost in which this first community waited and prayed for the descent of the Holy Spirit. It is the pattern for how we should spend these special days before Pentecost.

The following prayer is offered as a suggestion to aid the reader in his or her own prayerful preparation for Pentecost:

> **Holy Spirit**—whom the loving Father sends us in Jesus' name; Spirit of truth, love, and power. I adore You!

> **Come, Spirit of Truth**—lead us deeper into the truth of our faith (Jn 6:13). Give us humble, open hearts—you who alone knows what lies at the depth of God (1 Cor 2:11), reveal God to us; help us to recognize the gifts he has given us; give us true, strong, deep supernatural faith. By your grace may we adore Jesus as Lord (1 Cor 12:23) and be his effective witnesses (Acts 1:8).

> **Come, Spirit of Love**—dwell in us powerfully—fill us with divine love, free us from fear (Rom 8:15), and deepen our joyful sense of adoption and intimacy with the Father (Gal 4:6). Draw us to ardent love for Jesus;

suffuse all our affections with your divine grace, submerging them in the love of God.

**Come, Spirit of Power**—help us in our weakness; give us the grace we need for the work you have called us to do; make us strong, loving, and wise (2 Tim 1:7). Help us look forward in hope to our resurrection that you will effect (Rom 8:11) and to the glory of heaven; may we seek what is above and not what is on earth; may we store up treasure in heaven; bring us through a holy death to the vision of God.

We ask all this in Jesus' name.

Mary, Queen of the Upper Room, who waited with the disciples for the coming of the Spirit—lend your intercession to ours and ask the Holy Spirit to come to us this Pentecost and fill us with his Love.

Amen.

# $\mathcal{P}$entecost

✤

## Historical Background

On the fiftieth day after Passover (fifty days: *Pentecosta* in Greek), the Jews celebrated a festival of thanksgiving for the year's harvest (see Lev 23:15–23). Later it became a day to recall the giving of the Law to Moses on Mount Sinai in a theophany that involved wind and fire. For the Jews the slaying of the sacrificial lamb at Passover and the giving of the Law on Mount Sinai solidified the old covenant. Likewise, for Christians the death of Christ, the true paschal lamb (1 Cor 5:7) and the descent of the Spirit fifty days later began the new covenant. Pope St. Leo the Great writes:

> For as of old, when the Hebrew nation was released from the Egyptians, on the fiftieth day after the sacrificing of the lamb, the Law was given on Mount Sinai, so after the suffering of Christ wherein the true Lamb of God was slain . . . the Holy Spirit came down . . . the

second covenant was founded by the same Spirit who had instituted the first. (Sermon 75)

## Reflections

### I.

*"The love of God has been poured out into our hearts through the holy Spirit that has been given to us." (Rom 5:5)*

The entire Paschal Mystery of Jesus, his self-emptying, obedience, painful sufferings and death, resurrection, and ascension, are one great drama of his love for the human race that reaches its culmination in his pouring out of the Holy Spirit on us today. This is how one twelfth-century Cistercian abbot explained it to his monks:

> How ineffable is God, how unutterable his mercy. The esteem in which the divine love holds us is completely inexpressible. It was not enough for the Father to have given his Son to redeem a slave unless he were to give the Holy Spirit also, through whom he adopts the slave as his own! He gave his Son as the price of redemption; he gave the Spirit as the bill of adoption. O God, you lavish yourself on man far beyond his dreams. . . . Just as he did not spare his own Son but gave him up for us all, so also he has not spared the Holy Spirit, but he has poured him out on all flesh with a liberality of a new and astonishing depth.[1]

A modern renowned theologian expresses similar sentiments about the result of our possession of the Spirit:

> God is ours. He has not given us merely a gift. No, he has given us his whole being without reserve: he has given us the clarity of his knowledge, the freedom of his love, and the bliss of his Trinitarian life. He has given us himself. And his name is Holy Spirit. He is ours. He is

in each heart that calls to him in humble faith. He is ours to such an extent that, strictly speaking, we can no longer say what man is if we omit the fact that God himself is man's possession. God is our God: that is the glad tidings of Pentecost—the message that God loves us and has blessed us with himself.[2]

The Spirit comes to us as our companion, our friend, our helper. Jesus tells his followers that in a certain way the Spirit takes his place: "I tell you the truth, it is better for you that I go. For if I do not go, the Advocate will not come to you. But if I go, I will send him to you" (Jn 16:7).

Some saints have seen the Spirit as a sort of maternal presence of God towards us. St. Teresa Benedicta of the Cross (Edith Stein) wrote of the Holy Spirit:

> Sweet light—you lead me like a mother's hand, and should you let go of me, I would not know how to take another step. You, nearer to me than I am to myself and more interior than my most interior, and still impalpable and intangible and beyond any name: Holy Spirit— eternal Love!

As the Blessed Trinity is ineffably united in a single Godhead, the Holy Spirit does not really replace Jesus but rather brings us into a more dynamic union with him. He enables us to worship and trust him: "No one can say, 'Jesus is Lord,' except by the holy Spirit" (1 Cor 12:3). It is the Holy Spirit who unites us to the Mystical Body of Christ (1 Cor 12:13) and makes us living branches on the Vine that is Christ (Jn 15).

## 2.

*"Come, Holy Spirit, and kindle in the hearts of all the faithful the fire of your love!"*

What is the work of the Holy Spirit in us? It is the Holy Spirit who gives us the joyful confidence of being the adopted children of God the Father. St. Paul makes this clear to the Galatians when he writes: "As proof that you are children, God sent the spirit of his Son into our hearts, crying out, 'Abba, Father!'" (Gal 4:6). The word "Abba" is the original Aramaic expression a child uses towards its natural father.

It is the divine sonship that is the source of the life of grace in us. The Holy Spirit unites us to Christ so that what he is by nature we share by grace. Being each united to Christ by the Spirit we form, as it were, one great Mystical Body of Christ—all being different members but all sharing the one life of Christ by grace. It is the Spirit who unites us not only to Christ but to one another and who leads, directs, and vivifies the whole body of Christ. For this reason the Holy Spirit has been called "the soul of the Church."

As is clear from the New Testament, the early Church was very conscious of the presence and action of the Holy Spirit as the source of all of its holiness, gifts, and apostolic progress. In our own day this consciousness is happily being restored and spread among our people. The growth of charismatic prayer groups and the presence of many works of the Spirit both within and outside such groups has stirred the faith and love of many towards the person of the Holy Spirit once again. This is a reemphasis on a most authentic and essential dimension of the faith and a cause for great satisfaction.

As we attempt to discern the presence and action of the Spirit in the Church and our own lives, we must be humble and do so in the context of time given to serious and pro-longed prayer. The action of the Spirit is not always what we expect it to be. As noted above, recent years have given ample example of new directions in which the Spirit is lead-ing the people of God that were not the results of anyone's careful calculations or theological conclusions. We know that the Spirit remains with the Church sustaining in it a dynamic unity enriched with gifts and preserved by the apostolic office and other ministries. The presence of the Spirit is the source of our confidence and optimism despite all the possibilities of human failings.

In our personal lives, too, we can be confident of the help of the Holy Spirit if we surrender ourselves to his work. Often, however, we may not be aware of his work because we are looking for it in the wrong place. We expect the Holy Spirit to free us from the darkness of faith or the self-dying of Christian love, from the purification of patient waiting or the endurance of refining temptation, from the physical, mental, and spiritual stress of everyday life. Those are false expectations of God's Holy Spirit, and we will not find him active as the servant of our self-love.

While the Holy Spirit will on occasion bestow a consoling realization of God's love, the tradition of the Church and the example of the saints indicate that he will more often enable us to follow Christ on his path of selfless love and service to God the Father and his fellow human beings. And so the third person of the Holy Trinity will be for us the Spirit of faith in darkness, the Spirit of freedom in obedience and self-sacrifice, the Spirit of joy in our tears and suffering, the Spirit of eternal life in the midst of death.

The feast of Pentecost refocuses our gaze then on the Person of the Holy Spirit, our adorable and ever-present divine helper to whom is due every day of the year our adoration, love, reverence, and confidence. Let us make our daily prayer that of the liturgy of Pentecost: "Come, Holy Spirit, and kindle in the hearts of all the faithful the fire of your love!"

## 3·

*"He breathed on them and said to them, 'Receive the holy Spirit.'"*
*(Jn 20:22)*

Pentecost is "the birthday of the Church," not only in its invisible and mystical reality as noted above, but also in its visible institutional manifestation. We can never separate the Church from the Holy Spirit.

In today's gospel reading we hear Jesus' words: "'As the Father has sent me, so I send you.' And when he had said this, he breathed on them and said to them, 'Receive the holy Spirit'" (Jn 20:21–22). Today's first reading from the Acts of the Apostles describes the first public preaching of the gospel to the people in Jerusalem on Pentecost day. Acts goes on to narrate the Spirit-filled proclamation made by Peter, the chief shepherd of this community coming into being:

> God raised this Jesus; of this we are all witnesses. Exalted at the right hand of God, he received the promise of the holy Spirit from the Father and poured it forth, as you [both] see and hear. . . . Therefore let the whole house of Israel know for certain that God made him both Lord and Messiah, this Jesus whom you crucified. (Acts 2:32–36)

As the Acts of the Apostles unfolds we see the newly empowered Christian community growing into the Spirit-guided institutional Church. Constantly the decisions of the pastors are inspired by the Holy Spirit (see, e.g., Acts 10). In resolving the first major crisis in the early Church over the reception of gentile converts into the community the apostles said: "It is the decision of the holy Spirit and of us not to place on you any burden beyond these necessities" (Acts 15:28). Pope Benedict XVI speaks of a "compenetration" of the Holy Spirit and the institutional Church. Jesus had said:

> When the Advocate comes whom I will send you from the Father, the Spirit of truth that proceeds from the Father, he will testify to me. And you also testify, because you have been with me from the beginning. (Jn 15:26)

There is therefore a mysterious fusion of the divine and human witness, and from this flows the Church's chief work of evangelization begun on the day of Pentecost and entrusted to the Church as its task and mission. The Spirit continues to lead the Church in this enterprise that still has a long way to go to completion until the Lord's return.

On this day we should pray to the Holy Spirit to energize the Church anew for its mission and to stir up a true missionary spirit in ourselves and the whole Church community. In the power of the Holy Spirit we should be willing to speak up for our faith and defend it against its persecutors. The mission of evangelization belongs to all. Our faith is not a private possession for our personal comfort but a treasure to be shared.

Finally this great solemnity should fill us and the whole Church with an abiding spirit of peace, hope, and joy. The words Paul addresses to the community of Rome are spoken to us as well:

> May the God of hope fill you with all joy and peace in believing, so that you may abound in hope by the power of the holy Spirit. (Rom 15:13)

# $\mathcal{T}$rinity Sunday

✤

## Historical Background

With Pentecost, our annual celebration of the entire mystery of Christ is completed and we return to ordinary time until Advent. Interestingly, the Eastern Churches observe the Sunday after Pentecost as the feast of All Saints. The work of the Holy Spirit in the hearts of Christ's followers, transforming and sanctifying them, is celebrated on this day. In the Western Church, however, this Sunday is kept as a special day in honor of the Blessed Trinity. This custom began only around the beginning of the second millennium:

> Stephen, Bishop of Liege, solemnly instituted the Feast of the Holy Trinity for his Church in 920. . . . The Cistercian Order, which was spread through Europe, had ordered it to be celebrated in all its houses as far back as 1230. . . . Pope John XXII in 1334 extended its observance to all Churches.[1]

Having seen the loving and saving work of God unfold
from the Advent of Christ, through his Paschal Mystery, to
the sending of the Spirit, the Church now feels compelled to
turn to this One Saving God in his Divine Essence and offer
a tribute of praise, adoration, glory, and thanksgiving. The
various prayers of today's feast reflect this intention and
worship. It is very much a feast of pure worship of the mystery of God—one and three, the Blessed Trinity.

## Reflections

---

### I.

### "God is love." (1 Jn 4:16)

St. Augustine spent fifteen years writing his great treatise
on the Trinity. He was never quite satisfied with what he
expressed and that is fitting, for the mystery of God utterly
transcends our human capabilities. Our best response is
one of silent adoration and love.

Yet, the human mind seeks some glimpse of understanding of this central mystery of our faith. Augustine found his
best insight by focusing on the words of St. John: "God is
love" (1 Jn 4:16). Within God is an infinite ocean of love, and
this suggested to Augustine the inevitability of Trinity:
"Love means someone loving something loved with love.
There you are with three, the lover, what is being loved, and
love."[2] The Father is the lover, the Son is the beloved, and
the Spirit is the love that unites them. Augustine writes:
"Embrace love which is God and embrace God with love."
For Augustine, echoing St. John, this Triune love has to over-
flow into mutual love for our brothers and sisters, which
then is a reflection of Trinitarian love:

> "Beloved, let us love each other because love is from
> God, and everyone who loves is born of God and
> knows God. Whoever does not love does not know
> God, because God is love"(1 Jn 4:7). This passage shows

clearly and sufficiently how this brotherly love—it is of course brotherly love that we love each other with—is proclaimed on the highest authority not only to be from God but also simply to be God. When therefore we love our brother out of love, we love our brother out of God; and it is impossible that we should not love especially the love that we love our brother with. Thus we infer that those two commandments cannot exist without each other: because God is love the man who loves love certainly loves God; and the man who loves his brother must love love. And that is the reason for what he goes on to say a little later: "Whoever does not love the brother whom he sees cannot love God whom he does not see" (1 Jn 4:20); for the cause of his not seeing God is that he does not love his brother. Whoever, you see, does not love his brother is not in love, and whoever is not in love is not in God, because God is love (1 Jn 4:8).[3]

Humanity is created in the image of God who is Love—One and Triune. That is why the human family is such a sacred reality for believers: a Father reflects the paternity of God, a Mother reflects the love of the Holy Spirit, children reflect the Eternal Son. The human family is an icon of God!

### 2.

*"God is not a sealed fortress . . . but a house full of open doors, through which we are invited to walk."*

One of the more intriguing representations of the Trinity is the icon painted by Andrew Rublev in 1425 for a Russian church. In it three angelic figures are seated around a table facing each other. The center space is vacant, seeming to invite the viewer to take a place. Contemplating this icon, Fr. Henri Nouwen observed:

As we place ourselves in front of the icon in prayer, we come to experience a gentle invitation to participate in the intimate conversation that is taking place among the three divine angels and to join them around the table. The movement from the Father toward the Son and the movement of both Son and Spirit towards the Father become a movement in which the one who prays is lifted up and held secure.[4]

This contemplation helps us see and rejoice in the Catholic doctrine of grace in a new way. We see that grace is not a static supernatural entity, but rather is a relationship with the Persons of the Blessed Trinity. Indeed, one of the earliest expressions of this doctrine is expressed in a fully Trinitarian way: "As proof that you are children, God sent the spirit of his Son into our hearts, crying out, 'Abba, Father!'" (Gal 4:6).

Classical Catholic theology spoke of two "processions" in the Trinity: the Son from the Father and the Spirit from both. The end result of these processions is to bring us into this Trinitarian life, which we call being "in the state of grace."

Hans Urs von Balthasar eloquently develops this implication of the doctrine of the Trinity:

> The Father can give us the Son to be "with" us at a human level—the Son's eternal proceeding from the Father is continued in the dimension of time—but when the Son takes us with him into his communion ("being with") with the Father, he does so in a way that opens us to the cascading stream of life of the absolute "With," namely, the Holy Spirit. "If you knew the gift of God. . . . Whoever drinks of the water that I shall give him will never thirst; the water that I shall give him will become in Him a spring of water welling up to eternal life" (Jn 4:10, 14). God is not a sealed fortress, to be attacked and seized by our engines of war (ascetic practices, meditative techniques, and the like) but a house full of open doors, through which we are invited to walk.
>
> In the Castle of the Three-in-One, the plan has always been that we, those who are entirely "other," shall participate in the superabundant communion of life.[5]

## 3.

*"Adoration and love be to Thee, O perfect Trinity."*

Since this Sunday is especially a day for prayerful adoration, the following prayer adopted from Abbot Gueranger is offered to assist the reader in his or her own devotion:

**O Unity divine!** O Trinity divine! Bear with us while we dare to make our worship before Thee. Infinite God who has revealed Thyself—happy are we who can proclaim Unity and Trinity in Thine infinite Essence! Glory be to Thee, O Divine Essence that art but One! Thou art Being—infinite, necessary, perfect, peaceful, and sovereignly happy. In Thee we acknowledge three Persons—one same divine nature common to all.

**Glory be to Thee, O Father**—Ancient of Days; Unborn Thou beggetest from all eternity and so art eternally God and Father; Your Son has taught us that Thou art Father; we adore Thee; we love Thee as a Father should be loved by his children—all fatherhood is from Thee.

**Glory be to Thee, O Son,** O Eternal Word; Thou emanate from his divine essence; coming out of the divine essence Thou art co-eternal; in thee the Father made all things; You are the Mediator, Redeemer, and Savior of our lost human race.

**Glory be to Thee, O Holy Spirit**—who eternally emanate from Father and Son—Thou art Divine Love, living Love, personal Love, and Thou art sent to us as Friend and Helper.

**Adoration and love be to Thee, O perfect Trinity**—One God—Glory to Thee—may we see Thee face to face in a blissful eternity of love. Amen.[6]

# $\mathcal{B}$ody and Blood of the Lord

❧

## Historical Background

Around the beginning of the second millennium, Berengarius, a theologian of Tours, began promoting theories against the eucharistic presence of the Lord that were strongly contested by St. Norbert, founder of the Premonstratensian Canons. An increase of eucharistic piety was the result. A private revelation to a Belgian nun, Juliana of Mt. Cornillon, led to the introduction of a special feast in honor of the Body and Blood of the Lord in the diocese of Liege in 1246.

Pope Urban II, residing in Orvieto in Italy, where a eucharistic miracle had occurred, was inspired to extend this feast to the entire Church, which he did in 1264. St. Thomas Aquinas, who was serving in Orvieto as a theologian with the Papal court, was assigned to compose the Mass and Office used for this feast, including the special Sequence for the Mass and the hymns for Eucharistic Adoration and Procession.[1]

Reflections

---

I.

*"He became man that we might become gods!"*

The yearly cycle of the sacred liturgy above all else celebrates God's love. Having celebrated the mystery of our salvation in these past months we now see more clearly the ineffable love of God for his creatures. We have seen the sacrificial self-giving of the Son and the outpouring of the Spirit. It seems that God cannot do enough to prove his love and convince us of our dignity in his eyes. God is truly the Loving Shepherd of his people.

The ultimate purpose of all God's saving deeds is to elevate us to a status of adopted sons and daughters. The fathers of the Church often said of Christ: "He became man that we might became gods!" This is the divine life God wishes to share with us.

> God sent his Son, born of a woman, born under the law, to ransom those under the law, so that we might receive adoption. As proof that you are children, God sent the spirit of his Son into our hearts, crying out, "Abba, Father!" So you are no longer a slave but a child, and if a child then also an heir, through God. (Gal 4:4–7)

This awesome purpose and goal of God for us is realized and effected most concretely and tangibly for us in the sacrament we celebrate on this day—the sacrament of the Body and the Blood of the Lord:

> Whoever eats my flesh and drinks my blood remains in me and I in him. Just as the living Father sent me and I have life because of the Father, so also the one who feeds on me will have life because of me. (Jn 6:56–57)

The eucharist draws us, lowly and sinful creatures, directly into the divine life of the Triune God! This is the culmination of God's redeeming work and what we celebrate today with both solemnity and joy. Too often Catholics have only a moralistic understanding of their religion as a program of obligations and prohibitions. This shallow understanding of Christianity ignores the whole freedom from the slavery of the law noted above and our transformation into adopted children of God, co-heirs with Christ. On this great solemnity, then, let us hear anew the essence of our Christian faith:

> We have come to know and to believe in the love God has for us.
>
> God is love, and whoever remains in love remains in God and God in him. (1 Jn 4:16)

## 2.

### *"This is my body." (Mt 26:26)*

We believe in the true presence of the actual glorified body of Jesus Christ in this sacrament:

> The greatest mystery of the Christian faith is that God came to us in the body, suffered with us in the body, rose in the body, and gave us his body as food. No religion takes the body as seriously as the Christian religion. The body is not seen as the enemy or as prison of the spirit, but celebrated as the Spirit's temple. Through Jesus' birth, life, death, and resurrection, the human body has become part of the life of God. By eating the body of Christ, our own fragile bodies are becoming intimately connected with the risen Christ and thus prepared to be lifted up with him into the divine life. Jesus says, "I am the living bread which has come down from heaven. Anyone who eats this bread will live forever and the bread that I shall give is my flesh, for the life of the world." (Jn 6:51)

It is in union with the body of Christ that I come to know the full significance of my own body. My own body is much more than a mortal instrument of pleasure and pain. It is a home where God wants to manifest the fullness of the divine glory. This truth is the most profound basis for the moral life. The abuse of the body—whether it be psychological (e.g., instilling fear), physical (e.g., torture), economic (e.g., exploitation), or sexual (e.g., hedonistic pleasure seeking)—is a distortion of true human destiny: to live in the body eternally with God. The loving care given to our bodies and the bodies of others is therefore a truly spiritual act, since it leads the body closer towards its glorious existence.

The feast of the body of Christ is given to us to fully recognize the mystery of the body and to help us find ways to live reverently and joyfully in the body in expectation of the risen life with God.[2]

## 3.

*"We carry the sacrament through the fields and wilderness of our life."*

A special feature that characterizes this feast is the Solemn Eucharistic Procession in which the Blessed Sacrament is carried through the streets of cities and towns. Perhaps the most famous is the procession in Orvieto itself where the feast was first proclaimed. This two-hour procession carrying the monstrance and also the Miraculous Corporal of Bolsena winds through the streets of that hilltop town with many of the townspeople in medieval costumes. Significantly, it makes only two stops: one at the convent of the cloistered Carmelite nuns, who are not allowed to go out, and one at the local prison. In both cases the cardinal officiating carries the Lord into those dwellings for special prayers and blessings. The Eucharistic Lord comes to saints and sinners alike!

The meaning of the procession was described by Pope Benedict XVI in his homily on this feast in 2007:

> We join together this evening in the Procession to carry the Lord Jesus, as it were, to all the streets and neighborhoods of Rome. We bring him, as it were, into the ordinariness of our daily life, because he walks where we walk, because he lives where we live. We journey on the streets of this earth, knowing that he is at our side, sustained by the hope of one day seeing his unveiled presence in the final encounter of heaven.

Another great theologian has also eloquently written about the various meanings of the procession, and he is worth quoting at length:

> What is the first thing that the Corpus Christi procession tells us? It tells us—or rather through it we remind ourselves—that we are pilgrims on the earth. We have here no lasting dwelling place. We are a people who change, who are restlessly driven on through time and space, who are *in via*, and still seeking our real homeland and our everlasting rest. We are those who must allow themselves to be changed, because to be a member of the human race means to let oneself change, and perfection means to have changed often. The movement of the procession makes perfectly clear our dependence on time and the stratification of the sphere of our existence. But this procession is not merely a throng, and its motion is not only the mass flight of those who are hurrying through time and the barren desert of earthly existence. A procession is a holy movement of those truly united. It is a gentle stream of peaceful majesty, not a procession of fists clenched in bitterness, but of hands folded in gentleness. It is a procession which threatens no one, excludes no one, and whose blessing even falls on those who stand astonished at its edge and who look on, comprehending nothing. It is a movement which the holy One, the eternal One supports with his presence; he gives peace to

the movement and he gives unity to those taking part in it. The Lord of history and of this holy exodus from exile towards the eternal homeland himself accompanies the exodus. It is a holy procession, one that has a goal, both before it and with it. From this point of view, we can understand the specific significance of this procession.

It tells us of the eternal presence of human guilt in the history of mankind and in our own history; yes, even in the history of my life. With us on our march we carry the Body which was given for us. The Cross of Calvary goes with us, the sign that the guilt of deicide weighs upon mankind. The Body and the life that we all have crushed in death goes with us. This procession of sinners tells us that in our journey through time we always have the crucified One with us. When we walk down our streets, past houses where dwell sinful luxury, sinful misery, and darkness of hearts, then we are walking past new manifestations of sin of the world. When we walk right into the midst of these manifestations, then we are proclaiming his death, which we are all guilty of, and our death. Through this procession, which is accompanied by the crucified One, we acknowledge that we are sinners and that we have to suffer our own guilt and that of all mankind. We confess that again and again we walk down the path of error, of guilt, and of death, the path which the sinless One also walked for us and always continues to walk with us—in the Sacrament and in the grace of his Spirit. This path has mysteriously become redemption for those who believe with love, who understand this sacrament, and who take it with them on their dark path.

The procession also tells us of the abiding presence of Christ, our peace and reconciliation, on the paths of our life. He goes with us, he who is reconciliation, he who is love and mercy. During all the time that we call life, as we trudge along the streets of this earth, he is there, right behind us, pursuing us in the obstinacy of his love. He follows us, even when we walk a crooked path and lose our direction. He seeks the lost sheep even in the wilderness, and he runs to meet the prodigal son. He walks with us on the pilgrimage of our life, he who walked down all these streets himself—*quarens me sedisti lassus*—from birth to death. He therefore knows how we feel on this endless journey that is so often trackless. He is near at hand, visible and invisible, with the mercy of his heart, with the patient and full and merciful experience of his whole life. He, salvation itself, and the propitiation of our sin. We carry the sacrament through the fields and wilderness of our life, and give testimony that as long as he goes with us we have with us the one who can make every way straight and purposeful.

The procession also tells us of a blessed wonder: since the incarnation and death and resurrection of Christ, our movement in the procession is not only towards a goal, but we already move right in the midst of the goal itself. Indeed, the end of the age has already come over us. Yes, we wandering pilgrims already carry in our hands the one who is himself our end and our goal. We lift up the body, in which divinity and humanity are already indissolubly united. We carry the glorified body (although still hidden under the veils of this world) in which the world, in a moment that belongs to her forever, has already begun to be glorified and to tower up into the eternal, inaccessible light of God himself. The motion of the world, so the Corpus Christi procession tells us, has already entered upon its last phase, and as a whole it can no longer miss its goal. The distant goal of this motion of all millennia has already mysteriously penetrated into the movement itself. It is there not merely as promise and as a far distant future, but as reality and presence.[3]

# $\mathcal{S}$acred Heart of Jesus

❧

## Historical Background

Devotion to Jesus' humanity, focused on his heart as a symbol of his infinite and merciful love for humankind, flows easily from the scriptures themselves in which Jesus speaks of his meek, humble, and loving heart (Mt 11:29) as the place where we may find our deepest rest.

In the second millennium saints and mystics began to further explore this theme. St. Bernard, St. Anthony of Padua, St. Gertrude, and others all wrote beautifully on this subject, emphasizing the personal love of Christ for each person. In the seventeenth century—almost it would seem as a reaction to the severity of Jansenism—Jesus revealed this devotion in a special way to St. Margaret Mary Alacoque (1647–90), a cloistered Visitandine nun. Her revelations had a profound and positive effect on Catholic piety, and it is due to her mediation that this feast was instituted in response to the specific request of the Lord himself.

Reflections

---

## I.

*"Heart speaks to heart."*

Our keynote for this feast might well be John Henry Cardinal Newman's motto: *Cor ad cor loquitur,* or "Heart speaks to heart." This feast invites us to focus on the Sacred Heart of Jesus and also to look deeply into our own hearts and truly open them without fear and hesitation to the love of Christ.

The heart of Jesus—why this symbol, this devotion? The essence of God is his *hesed* (merciful love) and *hemeth* (faithful love), as the Old Testament scriptures ceaselessly proclaim. To give, however, our human nature a tangible and concrete sign of these divine qualities the Father ordained the pierced human heart of Jesus. We humans need this kind of visible, sacramental sign to attain to divine mysteries, to know the merciful and trustworthy love of God. His heart, as revealed to St. Margaret Mary, has flames of love leaping up from it and the wound of the spear that ended his life (Jn 19:34) and brought forth water and blood.

In his private revelations to St. Margaret Mary, Jesus said: "Behold this heart which has so loved men." These words are a faithful echo of the scripture texts that focus on the love of Christ:

> What will separate us from the love of Christ? Will anguish, or distress, or persecution, or famine, or nakedness, or peril, or the sword? As it is written:
>
> "For your sake we are being slain all the day; we are looked upon as sheep to be slaughtered."
>
> No, in all these things we conquer overwhelmingly through him who loved us. For I am convinced that neither death, nor life, nor angels, nor principalities, nor

present things, nor future things, nor powers, nor height, nor depth, nor any other creature will be able to separate us from the love of God in Christ Jesus our Lord. (Rom 8:35–39)

Christ's heart is a powerful sign and reminder of his merciful love. One thinks of Blessed Charles de Foucauld who never wrote a page in his notebook without putting the outline of the heart of Christ and the cross with the words "Jesus-Love." It became a synthesis for him of the whole Christian faith.

## 2.

*"Rejoice with me because I have found my lost sheep." (Lk 15:6)*

In our first reflection we discussed the heart of Jesus; but what about our own hearts, what role do they play in the celebration of this solemnity? It is significant that one of the gospels offered for this feast (Luke 15) recounts Jesus' image of himself as the Good Shepherd who goes in search of the straying sheep. Does this image reflect our hearts? The saints over the centuries have thought so:

Come Lord Jesus to look for your servant, to search for the tired sheep. Come, O Shepherd, and look for me. . . . Come with charity and gentleness of heart. . . . Come to look for me, for I too am seeking you. Search for me, find me, gather me to you, carry me! (St. Ambrose of Milan)[1]

St. Therese of Lisieux expresses similar sentiments:

I need a heart burning with tenderness who will be my support forever, who loves everything in me, even my weakness and who never leaves me day or night. I could find no human who could always love me and never die. I must have a God who takes on my nature and becomes my brother. . . . O heart of Jesus, You yourself are my happiness, my only hope.[2]

## 3.

*"I will rather boast most gladly of my weaknesses." (2 Cor 12:9)*

Perhaps the best road to spiritual growth is by humility, accepting the poverty of our hearts and then opening them to Christ. This was the experience of St. Paul: "I will rather boast most gladly of my weaknesses, in order that the power of Christ may dwell with me" (2 Cor 12:9). This has been well expressed by one Cistercian monk:

> The most difficult part of our ascesis is to see clearly over and over again the sad, boring truth of my sinfulness, my lostness. And having seen and known that painful, neuralgic reality all too well over and over again there and then to allow God in Christ in *questo momento* to gaze on me with love and exquisite tenderness. It seems utter madness to allow myself to be the object of Christ's love and attention precisely in that moment. It's the great reversal, the sublime trick of the monastic vocation—I thought I was coming here to gaze on Christ, but it is Christ Jesus the Lord himself who wants to gaze upon me in my lowliness and poverty. And even more than this, he invites me to believe that when I allow his gaze to rest on me, I actually console his sacred, wounded heart. It's wild, but it seems that's what he's telling us: "let me find you; let me carry you and gaze upon you." Our love consoles God in Christ. That's reason enough to celebrate our precariousness individually, communally, over and over again, day by day, even moment to moment.[3]

# Nativity of John the Baptist

---

## JUNE 24

⚜

## Historical Background

---

The birthday of the Baptist, the cousin of the Lord, was one of the earliest feasts with an established date in the liturgical calendar—indicating the prominence given to the immediate Precursor of the Lord by the early Church. In his homilies for the feast, St. Augustine notes that after the birthday of John the Baptist (near the summer solstice) the days begin to get shorter, whereas after the birth of Christ they get longer. Indeed, John the Baptist declared: "He must increase; I must decrease" (Jn 3:30). John's birth is celebrated as a holy event because the traditional interpretation of scripture is that he was already sanctified in the womb of Elizabeth, his mother, at the time of the visitation (Lk 1:14).

Reflections

---

### I.

*"Many will rejoice at his birth, for he will be great in the sight of [the] Lord." (Lk 1:14–15)*

John is the great "bridge figure" between the old and the new covenants. He comes as the last in the line of Hebrew prophets speaking in the Lord's name, and he is the first to acknowledge Jesus of Nazareth as the promised Messiah.

Jesus, Our Lord, gave the greatest tribute to John when he said: "Amen, I say to you, among those born of women there has been none greater than John the Baptist!" (Mt 11:11). His greatness is multifold:

> because of the special sanctifying grace given him in his mother's womb;

> because of the unique mission he had of introducing and baptizing Christ;

> because of the impression he made on Jews and Romans alike (Lk 3);

> because of his martyrdom for proclaiming the truth (Mt 14).

### 2.

*"Prepare the way of the Lord, / make straight his paths."*
*(Mk 1:3)*

We do not however honor John only as an important figure in the historical unfolding of Jesus' ministry—much less as a quaint archaic figure in his camel-hair robe and leather belt. John's impact is current and timeless:

> The Catholic cult of the saints is a bit more than an annual calling to mind of the holy—each annotated and featured as we would do for Lincoln or Washington on their birthdays. Our approach is more in the nature of a family reunion and the honored guest would be a living presence. We are in communion with the saints. All of us are united in the love of God and one another.
>
> The whole Christian thing has a sort of timelessness . . . our celebration of John the Baptist is no mere pausing in a busy week to think of him and his life and work. John is not gone—John lives. His ministry continues, Christianity is not a memory trip, a cult of the past. It is timeless. It all goes on now. [1]

What then might John's presence at our Catholic family gathering be calling us to at the beginning of the third millennium? May I suggest that John's call to us is very relevant in our day:

He is a son of the desert, a devotee of silence, solitude, and serious communion with God. In our modern noise-filled environment where the tools of instant communication fill our lives with no respite—"did you get my e-mail?"—John calls us to stop, pause, devote serious time daily to silence, prayer, communion with God—God alone!

In a culture of acquisitiveness, materialism, and indulgence John is calling us to sobriety and simplicity of lifestyle. He is telling us not to smother the longing for God in a welter of immediate tangible distractions and pleasures.

In a time when relativism is often seen as the only acceptable worldview, John calls us to be bold prophets of truth. As he confronted Herod because of his immoral lifestyle he calls us to be personally integral, to allow our faith and God's will to direct all our decisions and attitudes. He warns us against the tendency to "go along to get along" and urges us not to call the darkness light.

In these three ways especially, the great John the Baptist still says to us: "Prepare the way of the Lord, / make straight his paths" (Mk 1:3).

## 3.

*"[Elizabeth's] neighbors and relatives heard that the Lord had*
*shown his great mercy toward her, and they rejoiced with her."*
*(Lk 1:58)*

Even with these serious challenges to conversion, this feast
is a day of "joy in spirit" as the Opening Prayer affirms. We
are seeing in John's birth the great dawn of the mystery of
our salvation in Christ. In the second reading for today's
feast, Paul proclaims: "God, according to his promise, has
brought to Israel a savior, Jesus. John heralded his coming
by proclaiming a baptism of repentance" (Acts 13:23–24).

The gospel today (Lk 1:57–66) tells us that at the birth of
John neighbors and relatives "rejoiced with her"—
Elizabeth. This passage comes from the first two chapters of
Luke, which are filled with the joy and grace of salvation. It
is God's gift, sent in the person of his Son. The only possible
human response can be exultant joy and thanksgiving.

The second chapter of Luke contains the two chief
Christian prayers that the Church uses every day in the
liturgy of the hours: the Benedictus, which Zechariah,
John's father, prayed after John's birth, and the Magnificat,
which Mary prayed after she conceived Jesus.

Both Zechariah and Mary glorify God for his merciful
love to humanity. The core truth of our Christian faith is
that we too are loved and saved by God by his favor and
through no merit of ours. So the sentiments of these two
prayers should also be our deepest sentiments as we joyfully pray them each day. Today's feast calls us to recapture
this joy.

# Saints Peter and Paul

JUNE 29

## Historical Background

Peter and Paul were both martyred in Rome and buried there, most probably in the persecution of Nero (AD 59–68). Extensive excavations under St. Peter's Basilica have uncovered the "trophy of Gaius," a small monument over Peter's grave, which was placed in a pagan cemetery on the Vatican Hill across from the Tiber River and the inhabited part of ancient Rome.

Gaius refers to this "trophy" in a manuscript of AD 200 as something known to the Christians. After the Edict of Milan in AD 313, which gave Christians legal freedom, it was possible to honor the apostles in a more fitting way. Constantine, the first Christian emperor, leveled the Vatican Hill at the spot of Peter's grave and constructed a basilica there; he did the same at the site of St. Paul's tomb on the Ostian Way. The joint feast of Saints Peter and Paul on this day is very ancient, probably from the time of Constantine.

## Reflections

---

### I.

*"I live by faith in the Son of God who has loved me and given himself up for me." (Gal 2:20)*

Today we glorify and thank the Lord Jesus for the apostle Peter, the humble fisherman—the witness of key moments of Jesus' ministry, for example, the Transfiguration, the Agony in the Garden—who was made by Christ the rock foundation of his Church. We also glorify and thank the Lord for the apostle Paul—chosen and called by Christ to be the great proclaimer of the good news of the Son to the gentiles. Both were united in their ministry for Christ and in their martyrdom! They are truly "the founders of the Church" from whom we have received the beginning of the faith.

The essence of both their lives and ministry was their faith in Jesus, and so this is highlighted in today's gospel reading. Jesus asks "Who do you say that I am?" Often the disciples had asked him questions . . . now it is he who questions them. Peter speaks for them all: "You are the Messiah, the Son of the living God" (Mt 16:16).

So we are drawn today to meditate on this central reality of faith! We need to fully accept and embrace the mystery of faith—which is a gift of God. Our unaided human intellect cannot produce faith no matter how hard it tries:

> Peter and Paul could not know him except through the gift and grace of faith. Peter in today's Gospel, under the action of the Spirit, becomes a witness and a confessor of this superhuman truth (of Christ's divinity).

These words reveal the intimate truth of God, the very
life of God—Father and Son. No wonder Jesus exclaims
"Blessed are you, Peter!" Blessed because you could not
have humanly recognized this truth except by God's
action on you! (John Paul II, June 29, 2000)

Paul exclaims: "I live by faith in the Son of God who has
loved me and given himself up for me"(Gal 2:20). We consider today then the radically supernatural nature of
Christian faith. We receive and grow in faith by a humble
heart, willing to put aside our own presuppositions and
prejudices, and open to the wonders God's love can do.

## 2.

### *"Upon this rock I will build my church."*
### *(Mt 16:18)*

These words of today's gospel lead us also today to reflect
on the mystery of the Church. It is "built upon the foundation of the apostles" (Eph 2:20). It lives through the inheritance of Peter, the Petrine ministry of unity in the person of
the pope, and through the inheritance of Paul, the ceaseless
proclamation of the good news to all people.

It is God's plan that his saving love is to be mediated to
us through a community—the Church. We are not saved as
individuals but as members of a body, the body of Christ,
the Church. Just as our human life involves dependence on
others in a human family structure, so our spiritual life
involves dependence on others in the great family of faith
that is the Church.

The Church is often compared to Peter's boat—
battered by storms of history. It proclaims the gospel in a
hostile environment. The first and second readings of
today's Mass reflect the personal challenges and sufferings
Peter and Paul endured in their ministry. Yet both testify in
these two readings that the Lord never abandoned them
but was at their side. So he is with the Church in our day.

## 3.

*"Saints Peter and Paul . . . continue now and forever to protect this Church for which you lived and suffered."*

We might conclude our reflections with the following prayer for this feast composed by Pope Paul VI in the last year of his earthly life:

> Saints Peter and Paul, you brought the world the name of Christ and rendered to him the final witness of love and blood. Continue now and forever to protect this Church for which you lived and suffered. Keep her in truth and peace. Increase in all her children unshakeable loyalty to the Word of God, the sanctity of Eucharistic and sacramental life, serene unity in faith, concord in mutual charity, and constructive obedience to the Pastors. May she, the Holy Church, continue to be in the midst of the world the living, joyful, and active sign of God's redemptive plan and of his covenant with men. This is what she begs of you with the trembling voice of the lowly Vicar of Christ, who has looked to you, Saints Peter and Paul, as his exemplars and inspirers. So keep her with your intercession now and forever, until the final and beatifying encounter with the Lord who is coming. Amen, amen. (Paul VI, June 29, 1978)

# $\mathcal{T}$ransfiguration of Our Lord

---

## A U G U S T    6

❖

## Historical Background

---

This feast began in the Eastern Church, reflecting its more mystical theology and prayer. It was widely celebrated in the Byzantine Church on this day before the year 1000. The feast became obligatory in the West in 1456, in commemoration of a victory over the Turks in that year. One scripture scholar notes that "the feast of the Transfiguration was placed on this date in August to correspond more or less with a Jewish feast day of Moses' Transfiguration (Ex 34)."[1]

Reflections

---

I.

*"While he was praying his face changed in appearance and his*
*clothing became dazzling white." (Lk 9:29)*

A first approach to this beautiful mystery is suggested by
the great theologian, Fr. Karl Rahner, S.J. Using traditional
Ignatian meditation techniques, he suggests that we first
consider this event in terms of Jesus' own actual situation at
the time and thus seek to enter his mind and heart that we
might learn from him and come to share his sentiments.

Rahner points out that the arrangement of this episode
in all three synoptic gospels is important because this event
is always placed after the first announcement by Jesus of
his coming rejection, sufferings, and death. Despite all his
efforts, his journeys around the Holy Land, his tireless
preaching and many miracles, he has not provoked the
response of faith and conversion that is needed to prepare
for the coming of the kingdom of God. Instead, in many,
especially the leaders, he has provoked jealously, resent-
ment, and opposition. Rahner writes:

> We can get some sense of the sort of thoughts and feel-
> ings that might surely have filled the heart of the Savior
> as, with his three chosen apostles, he climbed a lone
> high mountain far from all people and their busy noise.
> It will surely have been the feeling of pain over the
> ingratitude, hardheartedness, and unbelief of his peo-
> ple, thoughts of his coming passion, readiness and
> resolve for the cross, but also anxiety and sadness.

> What does Jesus, then, do? He prays . . . he will have
> prayed to the Father for his unbelieving people, for his
> apostles and disciples, for faith and strength in the com-
> ing days of suffering. He will have said to his Father:

"See, I come to do your will. I am ready to drink this cup, to be baptized with the baptism of suffering."

No one goes unheard before the face of God. The Father hears the prayer of his much Beloved Son. Union with God, which Jesus otherwise holds hidden in the ultimate depths of his soul, now fills up all the chambers of his soul; it embraces his body, drawing it, too, into the blessedness of God's light. His face shone like the sun and his clothes were as radiant as light.

This then is the meaning of the transfiguration for Jesus himself: in the dark night of earthly hopelessness the light of God shines, a human heart finds in God the power which turns a dying into victory and into the redemption of the world.[2]

## 2.

*"This is my beloved Son. Listen to him."*
*(Mk 9:7)*

This is a Christological feast. The Spirit invites us also to go up the mountain of prayer today and hear anew the Father's witness to his Son. We are here at the heart of Christianity: the Father revealing the Son to us. "This is my beloved Son."

On this day then we might lay aside our burden of work projects, preoccupations, and troubles and give ourselves over to the contemplation and adoration of the Divine Son. We can be helped in this effort by the great proclamation of the first chapter of the Letter to the Hebrews, which powerfully expresses the mystery of Christ that is celebrated today and how he speaks God's word to us:

In times past, God spoke in partial and various ways to our ancestors through the prophets; in these last days, he spoke to us through a son, whom he made heir of all things and through whom he created the universe, who is the refulgence of his glory,

the very imprint of his being,

and who sustains all things by his mighty word.

When he had accomplished purification from sins,

he took his seat at the right hand of the Majesty on high,

as far superior to the angels

as the name he has inherited is more excellent than theirs.

For to which of the angels did God ever say:

"You are my son; this day I have begotten you"?

Or again:

"I will be a father to him, and he shall be a son to me"?

And again, when he leads the first born into the world,
he says:

"Let all the angels of God worship him." (Heb 1:1–6)

Today therefore we adore the Son—God from God, the perfect representation of the Father's being, the image of God for us. In awe and wonder—like Peter, James, and John—we behold his glory and are drawn deeper into the awesome mystery of his Being, a mystery we can never fully penetrate or fathom, but only adore.

As we have noted above, Christianity, at its core, is a Person—the Incarnate Son of God, Jesus of Nazareth. All else takes its meaning from him. The Church is his body extended in space and time. And so Christological faith and adoration are at the center of our experience of faith. We need to take time to be with him and to "listen to him," as the Father tells us today. This is the principal grace of this feast.

# 3.

*"All of us, gazing with unveiled face on the glory of the Lord, are being transformed into the same image from glory to glory."*

*(2 Cor 3:18)*

This day is also a feast of joyful hope for us. The glory of Jesus manifested today on the mountain is ours to share. The Preface of today's Mass thanks the Father that "his glory shone from a body like our own, to show that the Church, which is the body of Christ, would one day share his glory."

As St. Paul reminds us in today's Office of Readings: "All of us, gazing with unveiled face on the glory of the Lord, are being transformed into the same image from glory to glory" (2 Cor 3:18). This is the daily mysterious process of grace working within us. This process will reach a glorious fulfillment:

> See what love the Father has bestowed on us that we may be called the children of God. Yet so we are. . . . We are God's children now; what we shall be has not yet been revealed. We do know that when it is revealed we shall be like him, for we shall see him as he is. (1 Jn 3:1–2)

Pope Paul VI, who died on this feast in 1978, highlighted this theme in an address he had written but did not deliver:

> We celebrate the transcendent destiny of our human nature, which Jesus assumed, in order to save us and make our glorification possible. His body transfigured before the astonished eyes of the apostles, is also our body called to glory. The light which engulfed him foretells our share of his splendor.

# $\mathcal{A}$ssumption of the Blessed Virgin Mary

❖

## Historical Background

A most ancient prayer to Mary (*Sub tuum Praesidium*) dating from the third century refers to her as "glorious" and as heeding our prayers from heaven. This early intuition blossomed into a liturgical feast that was already observed on August 15 before the Council of Ephesus (431) when Mary was formally recognized as "Mother of God."

This feast of Mary on this very day spread widely throughout the Christian world. The Eastern Church referred to it as the Dormition, the "falling asleep" of Mary, and depicted it in a popular icon with the risen Christ standing at Mary's bier holding her as an infant in his hands. The West tended to emphasize the glorious rising of Mary in her body up to heaven. In 1950 Pope Pius XII confirmed the devotion, faith, and practice of the Church by declaring the Assumption as a dogma of faith.[1]

## Reflections

---

### I.

*"But when the fullness of time had come, God sent his Son, born of a woman." (Gal 4:4)*

The origin of all devotion to Mary must go back to the divine plan of salvation itself—this is the foundation of our veneration for Mary, whose earthly life and mission was crowned by her glorious Assumption into glory to reign with the Divine Son she had conceived and borne in her womb. The divine plan of salvation hinged on the role of this privileged woman. God, with supreme love, chose this humble young maid of Nazareth to be the "gate of heaven," the one through whom the Eternal Son would become man as Savior of the human race. Upon her *fiat*, "Let it be done," depended the fulfillment of God's saving plan. All of humanity is in her debt.

Mary is the source, the Mother who brings the Christ into the world. She is God's first collaborator in the great plan of salvation. She is at the center of the destiny of redeemed humanity. It is precisely because of her and her unique role in the Incarnation that the Church from the beginning has shown her extraordinary veneration.

The Assumption seems for these reasons a logical and fitting climax to Mary's union with her Divine Son from the beginning. As she made possible the Incarnation and stood at the foot of the cross, it is fitting that she should share in the total victory over sin and death that he effected by his Paschal Mystery.

## 2.

*"Your body, vessel that contained God, could not possibly suffer dissolution."*

In the Eastern Church, the feast we celebrate today is called the Dormition, literally the "falling asleep," of Mary. This means that at the end of her pilgrimage of faith Mary experienced death—but not a death like ours, for she was taken body and soul to heaven. We therefore thank the Father today because "You would not allow decay to touch her body for she had given birth to Your Son, the Lord of life." She is the Mother of life! St. Germanus of Constantinople wrote of Mary: "Your body, vessel that contained God, could not possibly suffer dissolution—how could you turn to dust and ashes who freed mankind from death through the flesh taken from you?"

Cardinal John Henry Newman offered these reflections on the mystery of the Assumption:

> I think its probability grows on the mind contemplating it steadily. It is in harmony with the doctrine of the Incarnation—without it Catholic teaching would have a character of incompleteness . . . it became Our Lord to raise his mother, and her so sinless . . . it is more difficult not to believe the Assumption than to believe it after the Incarnation. Mary is the second Eve—Eve would not have seen death or corruption if she had not sinned—so Mary did not see corruption because she had more than the prerogative of Eve.

We can therefore understand the words of St. Bernard in a homily for this feast:

> Dearest brethren, this time is a time when all flesh should shout for joy, because the Mother of the Word made flesh is assumed into heaven; nor should human mortality desist from singing songs of praise on this glorious festival, when the nature of man is elevated in

the Virgin to solitary eminence, high above all the
orders of immortal spirits.

## 3.

*"My soul proclaims the greatness of the Lord; / my spirit rejoices in
God my savior." (Lk 1:46–47)*

On this solemnity, the gospel that is proclaimed is Mary's
prayer—the Magnificat (Lk 1:46–55). Pope Benedict XVI
underlined the contemporary relevance of this prayer in the
homily he delivered on August 15, 2005:

> "Magnificat," my soul "magnifies" the Lord, that is,
> "proclaims the greatness " of the Lord. Mary wanted
> God to be great in the world, great in her life, and pres-
> ent among us all. She was not afraid that God might be
> a "rival" in our life, that with his greatness he might
> encroach on our freedom, our vital space. She knew that
> if God is great, we too are great. Our life is not
> oppressed but raised and expanded; it is precisely then
> that it becomes great in the splendor of God.

> The fact that our first parents thought the contrary was
> the core of original sin. They feared that if God were too
> great, he would take something away from their life.
> They thought they could set God aside to make room
> for themselves.

> This is also the great temptation of the modern age, of
> the past centuries. More and more people have thought
> and said: "But this God does not give us our freedom;
> with all his commandments, he restricts the space of
> our lives. So God has to disappear; we want to be
> autonomous and independent. Without this God we
> ourselves would be gods and do as we pleased."

> Only if God is great is humankind also great. With
> Mary, we must begin to understand that this is so. We
> must not drift away from God but make God present;

we must ensure that he is great in our lives. Thus, we too will become divine, all the splendor of the divine dignity will then be ours.

# $\mathcal{N}$ativity of the Blessed Virgin Mary

## SEPTEMBER 8

✤

## Historical Background

This feast was already being kept in the Eastern Churches when Pope St. Sergius mandated it for the Church of Rome in AD 701. Its earliest origins may have been in connection with the dedication of a church in Jerusalem to Saints Joachim and Anna, parents of Mary.

## Reflections

---

I.

*"Your birth, O Virgin Mother of God, proclaims joy to the whole world."*

A strong grace of this feast is to open ourselves to the joy of salvation. Mary's birth is, in a real sense, the dawn of a new age for humankind. The antiphon in the morning prayer Office for the canticle of Zechariah highlights this emphasis: "Your birth, O Virgin Mother of God, proclaims joy to the whole world, for from you arose the glorious Sun of Justice, Christ our God." This theme is also expressed in the Responsorial Psalm:

> With delight I rejoice in the Lord.
> Lord, I trust in your merciful love.
> Let my heart rejoice in your saving help.
> Let me sing to the Lord for his goodness to me,
> singing psalms to the name of the Lord.

St. Augustine developed this theme:

> With greatest exaltation our earth should rejoice at the birth of such a Virgin. Eve brought us tears; Mary brings us joy. Eve wounded our human nature, Mary has healed it; the faith of Mary has compensated for the unbelief of Eve. Eve brought mourning into the world, Mary has brought singing—"My soul magnifies the Lord."

St. John Damascene strikes a similar chord:

> Come one and all—let us joyfully celebrate the birth of the joy of all the world: This day is the beginning of the world's salvation. Mary is that virginal door from which and through which God is about to make his bodily appearance on earth. Today a branch from

Jesse's stump has sprouted from whom will be born the flower substantially united to divinity. Today on earth he who created the firmament has created a heaven—this heaven is far more splendid then the first.

## 2.

*"She will bear a son and you are to name him Jesus, because he will save his people from their sins." (Mt 1:21)*

The gospel of the genealogy of Jesus (Mt 1:1–23) is used on this feast. This gospel with its long list of strange sounding names reminds us powerfully about Jesus' human origins. Through Mary he becomes a member of the human race with a true human ancestry. Matthew presents Jesus as the Son of Abraham and traces his origins through generations of Jewish figures—some not so admirable in their conduct. Monsignor Romano Guardini, commenting on this passage, writes:

> St. Paul says of the Lord: "For we have not a high priest who cannot have compassion on our infirmities, but one tried as we are in all things except sin" (Heb 4:15). He entered fully into everything that humanity stands for—and the names in the ancient genealogies suggest what it means to enter into human history with its burden of fate and sin. Jesus of Nazareth spared himself nothing. In the long quiet years in Nazareth, he may well have pondered these names. Deeply he must have felt what history is, the greatness of it, the power, confusion, wretchedness, darkness, and evil underlying even his own existence and pressing him from all sides to receive it into his heart that he might answer for it at the feet of God.[1]

Mary's Son is truly one of us. On this day when we celebrate her birth, we are powerfully reminded that our Christian faith does not help us escape from the gritty realities of human life but immerses us more deeply in them.

The sinners and scoundrels in Jesus' own human lineage help us understand the need for those other words of today's gospel: "She will bear a son and you are to name him Jesus, because he will save his people from their sins" (Mt 1:21).

## 3.

*"She has given birth to the Child who created all things, even the Mother herself."*

Celebrating Mary's birth not only elicits true spiritual joy as noted above, but it also underlines the intimate and inseparable connection between the Mother and the Son-Savior. Mary's role is altogether unique in the economy of salvation.

This aspect of today's feast is highlighted by one of the great Cistercian Fathers—Guerric, Abbot of Igny, France— in his homily for this day:

> Today we celebrate the birthday of the Blessed Virgin Mother from whom the Life of all things took his birth. Today is the birthday of that Virgin from whom the Savior of all men willed to be born in order that he might give to all who were born to death the power to be reborn to life. Today is the birthday of that new Mother who has destroyed the curse brought by the first mother so that all those who through the fault of the first had been born under the yoke of eternal condemnation might instead, through her, inherit a blessing. She is indeed the new Mother, for she has brought new life to her children already hardening with age and has healed the defect of both inborn and acquired senility. Yes indeed. She is the new Mother, who by an unheard of miracle has given birth in such a way that, becoming a mother, she has not ceased to be a Virgin. And she has given birth to the Child who created all things, even the Mother herself.[2]

The spiritual consequence of these truths is that a trusting devotion to Mary should be a hallmark of every Christian—as it clearly has been of the saints from the beginning. No one has more at heart the success of her Son's saving work in us than Mary. We should daily entrust ourselves to her maternal care, that the full power of Christ's life in us may grow and transform us into his likeness and into witnesses to his love in the world.

As one of the more famous prayers to her, the Memorare, says:

> Remember, O Most gracious Virgin Mary, that never was it known that anyone who fled to your protection, implored your help, or sought your intercession, was left unaided. Inspired with this confidence, I fly unto you, O Virgin of virgins, my Mother.
>
> To you I come, before you I stand, sinful and sorrowful. O Mother of the World Incarnate, despise not my petitions, but in your mercy hear and answer me. Amen.

# *E*xaltation of the Holy Cross

---

## SEPTEMBER 1 4

✤

## Historical Background

---

A combination of historical events is commemorated by this feast, which is shared by the Churches of the East and West. First, it recalls the dedication in the fourth century of the church built in Jerusalem under the inspiration of St. Helena, mother of Constantine, to mark the spot of Jesus' crucifixion and burial—the Basilica of the Holy Sepulcher. This followed the finding of the remains of the cross on Calvary's hill. A later historical event is also enfolded in this feast—in AD 614 the Byzantine Emperor Heraclius recovered from the Persians relics of the cross that they had confiscated fifteen years earlier. They were returned to Jerusalem with great exultation and veneration.

## Reflections

---

### I.

*"May I never boast except in the cross of our Lord Jesus Christ."*
*(Gal 6:14)*

Spiritually and theologically, the focus of this feast is the joyful acknowledgment of the saving graces that have flowed to humanity through the sufferings and death of Christ. In contrast to a Lenten observance, which might focus more on the suffering dimension, this feast, which is celebrated in the red vestments of triumph, rejoices in the superabundant fruits of the cross—Christ's victory over sin, evil, and death—which are now shared in by the human family. The tone of this feast is set by the entrance antiphon adopted from Paul's Letter to the Galatians: "We should glory in the cross of Our Lord Jesus Christ for he is our salvation, our life, and our resurrection; through him we are saved and made free!"

Pope Paul VI expressed this dimension when he wrote:

> The Second Vatican Council brought into our common ecclesial vocabulary the phrase "the Paschal Mystery"—which is what we really celebrate in the Exaltation of the Cross. This means the Christian Passover, the passing of the Lord Jesus from death to life, from earthly existence to eschatological existence. The cross alone then does not describe the whole reality of salvation—it requires also the victory and the triumph of Christ.

> The cross occupies the visible and decisive side of the mystery: It represents the encounter of guilt with innocence; the clash between cruelty and goodness; the duel between life and death; the union of justice and mercy; the triumph of love in sacrifice.

It is then the triumph of Jesus on the cross that is celebrated on this day. As a symbol of the rich fruitfulness of the cross, Eastern Christians bless and distribute fragrant basil leaves on this day. The scriptures beautifully express this dimension:

> We do see Jesus "crowned with glory and honor" because he suffered death, he who "for a little while" was made "lower than the angels," that by the grace of God he might taste death for everyone. (Heb 2:9)

## 2.

*"Whoever wishes to come after me must deny himself, take up his cross, and follow me." (Mk 8:34)*

This feast is also an occasion for us to reflect on the role of suffering and the cross in our own lives. In our modern secular, hedonistic culture there is a great danger that, in St. Paul's words, "the cross of Christ be emptied of its meaning" (1 Cor 1:17).

For many moderns the crucified Christ is again "a scandal" and "foolishness," as Paul observed in his time in his First Letter to the Corinthians. Unbridled selfishness and self-indulgence is an unfortunate characteristic of much of modern society, as it was then. In this context we can hear again the words of Paul:

> For many, as I have often told you and now tell you even in tears, conduct themselves as enemies of the cross of Christ. . . . Their God is their stomach; their glory is in their "shame." (Phil 3:18–19)

Thus, Jesus' challenge to his followers is clear:

> Whoever wishes to come after me must deny himself, take up his cross, and follow me. For whoever wishes to save his life will lose it, but whoever loses his life for my sake and that of the gospel will save it. (Mk 8:34–35)

## 3.

*"Take my yoke upon you and learn from me, for I am meek and
humble of heart." (Mt 11:29)*

Christian faith calls forth the noblest and most generous
impulses of the human spirit. The martyrs, who gave their
lives over the centuries out of love for God, are the true
Christian heroes. To us, however, who may tremble before
the prospect of suffering and the cross in our lives, Jesus
gives the reassuring promise: "Take my yoke upon you and
learn from me, for I am meek and humble of heart; and you
will find rest for yourselves. For my yoke is easy, and my
burden light" (Mt 11:29–30).

What makes the yoke of the cross light is love. It is love
that can transform our sufferings from being an irritating
and vexing burden to being "salvific." Christian faith holds
that there is a mysterious saving power in suffering freely
accepted in love. Jesus' own cross is the paradigm. He
accepted every form of human suffering—physical, mental,
emotional—and made it a redemptive oblation for the
whole human race because he suffered it all with love, a
love that led him to choose from all eternity to be the means
of the reconciliation of sinful humans with God.

We too have the possibility to make our sufferings
redemptive and salvific. If we embrace them with love and
trust, patterned on Christ, we can make our own Paul's
words:

> Now I rejoice in my sufferings for your sake, and in my
> flesh I am filling up what is lacking in the afflictions of
> Christ on behalf of his body, which is the church. (Col 1:24)

# Archangels Michael, Gabriel, Raphael, and All the Angels

✤

## Historical Background

The origins of this feast seem to be found in a celebration of the consecration of a basilica in honor of St. Michael the Archangel on the Salarian Way near Rome. It is an ancient feast, having been kept on this day since the sixth century. In many ancient calendars, and especially in monastic ones, it was observed as a feast in honor of all the angels. After the Second Vatican Council the three archangels who previously each had his own feast were united on this one day. A special memorial of guardian angels is kept on October 2.

Reflections

---

## I.

*"The Son of Man will come with his angels in his Father's glory."*
*(Mt 16:27)*

Christ, Our Lord, clearly takes the existence of the angels for granted and not infrequently refers to them:

"The Son of Man will come with his angels in his Father's glory." (Mt 16:27)

"The angels will go out and separate the wicked from the righteous and throw them into the fiery furnace." (Mt 13:49)

"Whoever is ashamed of me and of my words, the Son of Man will be ashamed of when he comes in his glory and in the glory of the Father and of the holy angels." (Lk 9:26)

"But of that day or hour [of the end of the world], no one knows, neither the angels in heaven nor the Son, but only the Father." (Mk 13:32)

"See that you do not despise one of these little ones, for I say to you that their angels in heaven always look upon the face of my heavenly Father." (Mt 18:10)

In the early days of the Church the first disciples had a constant sense and awareness of the presence and help of these holy spirits: in the announcement by them of Jesus' resurrection (Mt 28; Lk 24); the freeing of the disciples from prison (Acts 5:19); the direction and inspiration given to the disciples by angels (Acts 10:3); the detailed account of Peter's rescue from Herod by his guardian angel (Acts 12).

Expressing the constant faith of the Church in 1215 the Fourth Lateran Council defined the existence of the angels. The *Catechism of the Catholic Church* (#328ff) repeats this teaching:

> The existence of the spiritual, non-corporeal beings that
> Sacred Scripture usually calls "angels" is a truth of

faith. The witness of Scripture is as clear as the unanimity of Tradition. . . . As purely spiritual creatures angels have intelligence and will: they are personal and immortal creatures surpassing in perfection all visible creatures. In her liturgy, the Church joins with the angels to adore the thrice-holy God.

**2.**

*"Their splendor shows us your greatness which surpasses in goodness the whole of creation."*

In addition to caring for and protecting us, the angels focus us on the greatness and wonderful power of God. In the Preface of this day we pray:

> In praising your faithful angels and archangels, we also praise your glory, for in honoring them we honor you, their creator. Their splendor shows us your greatness which surpasses in goodness the whole of creation.

God is infinitely greater and more wonderful than anything our narrow human mind can ever conceive. As the wonder of the visible universe—from the glory of the galaxies to the perfect order of every atom—leads us to glorify God, so our faith-knowledge about these good invisible spirits should also lead us to praise and glorify God, their Creator.

> The angels confirm us in the faith and increase our hope and love for God. This is not the least of the ways in which they accomplish their principal purpose: to praise with adoration their Infinite, Transcendent God, express their love and loyalty; this is their primary function, their joy supreme. To mediate in diverse manners His presence, His guidance, His power to all other creatures, especially to men: this is also their role in history.[1]

# 3.

*"To his angels he has given command about you, / that they guard you in all your ways." (Ps 91:11)*

In the midst of the uncertainties of human life, we can take great comfort from the truth that the very angels of God are our helpers and protectors:

> Are they not all ministering spirits sent to serve, for the sake of those who are to inherit salvation? (Heb 1:14)

Likewise, Psalm 91 reminds us that "to his angels [God] has given command about you, / that they guard you in all your ways" (v. 11).

One important way in which the angels guard us is by assisting in the spiritual struggle in which we are all engaged. The Office of Readings today features a mysterious showdown between St. Michael and those fallen angels who somehow rebelled against their Creator and are antagonists of those on the way to eternal salvation (Rev 12). The passage ends with the ominous words, "The dragon went off to make war on the rest of her offspring, those who keep God's commandments and bear witness to Jesus."

This struggle is part of our "faith vision of reality" and reflects the truth that both Peter and Paul already taught to the first Christians:

> Your opponent the devil is prowling around like a roaring lion looking for [someone] to devour. Resist him, steadfast in faith. (1 Pt 5:8)

> Put on the armor of God so that you may be able to stand firm against the tactics of the devil. For our struggle is not with flesh and blood but with the principalities, with the powers, with the world rulers of this present darkness, with the evil spirits in the heavens. (Eph 6:11–12)

Thus, in light of the above, one great theologian has drawn out some of the practical implications of this feast celebrated today:

> We should love the angels and pray to them often. God will ask an account of how we have appreciated this—among his other mercies—that he has bestowed on each of us an angel of his face—to help us on our journey back to him.[2]

# $\mathcal{A}$ll Saints

✤

## Historical Background

From the beginning of Christianity, the faithful instinctively sought the help of those who were with God. Inscriptions around tombs of the saints begged their prayers; as, for example, at the tomb of St. Peter the Apostle.

On this day in 609 Pope Boniface IV dedicated the Pantheon in Rome—a pagan temple—as a church in honor of Mary and All Martyrs. By AD 800 a feast of All Saints was widespread in Europe. Significantly, many Eastern Churches celebrate this feast on the Sunday after Pentecost, for it is the chief work of the Holy Spirit to make us saints.

## Reflections

---

### I.

*"Then I saw the heavens opened." (Rev 19:11)*

"I saw the heavens open"—these words of the Book of Revelation suggest a first area of reflection for this feast. It is the "feast of heaven" and invites us to rise above our daily routine, duties, and troubles and to focus on our ultimate goal and destiny—eternal life in heaven. Chapters 4 and 5 of the Book of Revelation present a powerful and dramatic vision of heaven with God the Father at the center:

> A throne was there in heaven, and on the throne sat one whose appearance sparkled like jasper and carnelian. Around the throne was a halo as brilliant as an emerald. . . . In front of the throne was something that resembled a sea of glass like crystal. (Rev 4:2–6)

Eternal worship ascends before God:

> Day and night they do not stop exclaiming:

> "Holy, holy, holy is the Lord God almighty, who was, and who is, and who is to come." (Rev 4:8)

At the center of the scene also is Jesus—described as "the Lamb that was slain." To him the saints all sing gratefully:

> With your blood you purchased for God
> those from every tribe and tongue, people and nation.
> You made them a kingdom and priests for our God,
> and they will reign on earth. . . .
> Worthy is the Lamb that was slain
> to receive power and riches, wisdom and strength,
> honor and glory and blessing. (Rev 5:9–11)

The author then describes the "great multitude" of saints "from every nation, race, people, and tongue" gathered before the throne of the Father and the Lamb:

> They stood before the throne and before the Lamb, wearing white robes and holding palm branches in their hands.
> They cried out in a loud voice:
> "Salvation comes from our God, who is seated on the throne, and from the Lamb." (Rev 7:9–10)

These inspired words of scripture use images and symbols to try to capture something of the awe and wonder of the eternal kingdom. It is important to note that the focus is on God; those who come into his presence are clearly full of joyful gratitude that he has saved them and made them saints.

Those who dwell in heaven experience total fulfillment and endless happiness. As one hymn expresses it:

> There the body has no torments, there the mind is free from care, there is every voice rejoicing, every heart is loving there.

So on this "festival of heaven" we do well to rekindle our hope in our ultimate destiny. Earthly life is but a pilgrimage on the way to the Father's house. From the perspective of heaven even our trials take on a different dimension:

> For this momentary light affliction is producing for us an eternal weight of glory beyond all comparison, as we look not to what is seen but to what is unseen; for what is seen is transitory, but what is unseen is eternal. (2 Cor 4:17–18)

## 2.

*"In the Church everyone is called to holiness."*
(Lumen Gentium, 39)

Our way to reach the kingdom is by holiness of life. Today then is also the "feast of holiness." Yet, we remember that Jesus alone is perfectly holy. Any holiness we may have is totally derived and received from him.

As the Dogmatic Constitution on the Church of the Second Vatican Council reminds us, "in the Church everyone is called to holiness" (*Lumen Gentium*, 39). This being the case, we cannot say that holiness is too utopian, too lofty, too difficult. Since God wills it for us, it must be accessible with God's grace. Often we have a distorted idea of holiness, imaging it must require constant exceptional feats of penance or extraordinary works of heroic charity. God may call some to express their holiness in that way. But for most of us holiness is a more mundane reality.

John Henry Cardinal Newman expressed well what holiness might involve for most of us:

> After the example of the saints our duty is to wait for the Lord's coming, to prepare the way before him, to pray that when he comes we may be found watching, to take up our cross meekly, to pray for all people. . . . May God give us the grace to do much and say little.[1]

In today's gospel, Jesus proclaims a "charter of holiness"— the Beatitudes, a way of life that makes sense only if one believes in and looks forward to a share in the kingdom of heaven. Jesus tells us that holiness involves being "poor in spirit," "meek and humble," "merciful," "pure of heart." These are all qualities we need in our ordinary daily life, for it is there that we find holiness. As the Second Vatican Council tells us, ultimately holiness is love:

> All Christians in any state or walk of life are called to the fullness of Christian life and to the perfection of

love, and by this holiness a more human manner of life is fostered also in earthly society. In order to reach this perfection the faithful should use the strength dealt out to them by Christ's gift, so that following in his footsteps and conformed to his image, doing the will of God in everything they may wholeheartedly devote themselves to the glory of God and to the service of their neighbor. (*Lumen Gentium*, 40)[2]

## 3.

*"We are surrounded by so great a cloud of witnesses."* (*Heb 12:1*)

On this day we celebrate what the Church calls "the communion of saints"—the truth that we are in a mysterious relationship with those who have gone before us. They care for us, pray for us, and can help us.

Dramatic evidence of this communion occurs in the process of canonizing new saints by the Church. Miracles are required to show the presence of the proposed saint in heaven and his or her intercessory power. On a daily and less tangible way we all have access to the friendship and assistance of the saints. In God's family we are all one.

On this day we remember those who have gone before us—parents, spouses, friends—who we pray are now with God. The "communion of saints" reminds us that they really are close to us and can help us. As we rejoice in their eternal happiness we can and should invoke them—the great saints of history, but also the less known, those dear to us. This should be a most comforting aspect of our Christian faith.

The galaxy of saints is wonderful—"men and women of every time and place"—husbands like Joachim, wives like Monica, young people like Aloysius, lawyers like Thomas More, doctors like Gianna Beretta Molla, bishops and priests, monks and nuns—even sinners who seem to have "stolen" heaven like St. Dismas, the "good thief." Yet, it is good to be reminded:

The Church of the Saints, though rejoicing in her proud heritage of saints in the past, looks with confident faith to the saints of the future. Magnificent saints are yet to appear: magnificent saints, are already in the making.

Beautiful and numerous as are the saints—those of bygone days and those of the present—the devout know that God has only begun the building of His kingdom on earth and that a thousand, ten thousand years hence the Church of the Saints will be immeasurably more glorious in the millions of saints who will follow out, in civilizations still undreamed, the imitation of the One and Only Perfect Saint, Our Lord Jesus Christ.[3]

# $\mathcal{D}$edication of the Lateran Basilica

## NOVEMBER 9

⚜

## Historical Background

In AD 313 the Roman emperor Constantine—himself a catechumen—gave Christians official legal freedom by a law known as the Edict of Milan. For the first time they could freely and publicly profess their religion. Subsequently, he personally donated land on the top of the Lateran Hill in Rome for the construction of a church. It was called the Basilica of Our Savior. Centuries later both St. John the Baptist and St. John the Evangelist were added as patrons. Today is celebrated as the anniversary of the dedication of the church by Pope St. Sylvester I (who reigned AD 314–35).

## Reflections

---

### I.

*"Do you not know that you are the temple of God, and that the Spirit of God dwells in you?" (1 Cor 3:16)*

A house is a place of refuge and of joy where a family gathers to show affection and support for one another, to share meals, to deepen bonds. In all these ways a house becomes a "home."

A church building is the House of God. It is where he welcomes his children to do all the same household things but in a deeper and more powerful way. It is where he builds his family, the Church. This is why we celebrate the anniversary of the dedication of a church.

In the church edifice God actually speaks to us in the liturgy of the word—he shares his vision of the human family, of reality, with us. He helps us understand our lives and destiny and how to live our lives as God's children in relationship to one another. We respond to God's word by faith and obedience, symbolized when we answer, "Thanks be to God" or "Praise to you, Lord Jesus Christ." In the church God also nourishes us with the banquet of heaven, the eucharist, supernatural food that gives us strength for the journey of life and that unites us to him in a most powerful way. God wants us to find joy, solace, and comfort in his house, a sense of being loved and of belonging to his family. The church is God's house and our spiritual home. It should be very special to us no matter how splendid or modest the physical edifice may be.

The Church surrounds the consecration of a church with exceptional solemnity. It has the bishop anoint its walls with sacred oil on twelve crosses that represent the Twelve Apostles upon whom, as scripture tells us, the Church is built. The altar is also anointed as the symbol of Christ, the cornerstone of the Church (1 Pt 2:4–8). All this reminds us that the church building is a symbol of a greater and deeper mystery: our being built up as a living temple for God to dwell in:

> Do you not know that you are the temple of God, and that the Spirit of God dwells in you? . . . The temple of God, which you are, is holy. (1 Cor 3:16–17)

### 2.

### *"Mother and Head of All Churches of the City and the World"*

The particular church honored today, the Lateran Basilica, is venerated because it is the cathedral of the Church in Rome—the pope's "Cathedra," or official chair. Its facade proudly bears a plaque hailing it as "Mother and Head of All Churches of the City (Rome) and the World." Every pope, shortly after his election, must go there to "take possession" of this church—the symbol of his special responsibility as bishop of Rome.

On this day, therefore, we celebrate the fact of our union with the bishop of Rome, the pope, and through him our union with the universal Church. The Catholic Church is a worldwide family of faith whose "Holy Father" is the pope. On this day we do well to pray for him and for his intentions as he seeks to shepherd the universal Church in the name of Christ:

> Jesus Christ put Peter at the head of the apostles, and in him he set up a lasting and visible source and foundation of the unity both of faith and communion. (*Lumen Gentium*, 18)

## 3.

*"You are 'a chosen race, a royal priesthood, a holy nation, a people of his own.'" (1 Pt 2:9)*

When Pope Sylvester had the opportunity to actually construct a Christian church building he had no precedent to go on. The decisions he made are very significant and afford us further material for reflection on this feast.

Pagan temples and even the Jewish Temple in Jerusalem were constructed around a very small enclosed *fanum*, a sacred space where only the chief priests had access to worship God. The people generally gathered in an open courtyard around the fanum, basically as spectators of the sacred worship enacted by the priests alone. Hence the term "profane" in our English language, meaning "outside the sacred."

Pope Sylvester, in designing the Lateran Basilica, created a revolution in the design of worship space, based on the true Christian understanding of all the baptized as a "royal priesthood" (1 Pt 2:9). His church allowed all the faithful to be inside, together as God's adopted children and sharers in the priesthood of Christ. While the ordained priest had a unique role in making present the Paschal Sacrifice of Christ, all the faithful were entitled to offer it to the Father as their own perfect worship of Almighty God.

On this feast of the dedication of this ancient Roman church we should all be full of grateful joy for the privilege that is ours as baptized believers. We might well echo the great prayer of thanks the Church uses for the Dedication of a Church:

> Father, all powerful, we give you thanks for this house
> of prayer in which you bless your family as we come to
> you on pilgrimage. Here you reveal your presence by
> sacramental signs, and make us one with you through
> the unseen bond of grace. Here you build your temple
> of living stones, and bring the Church to its full stature
> as the body of Christ.

# $\mathcal{T}$hanksgiving Day

---

❖

## Historical Background

---

In 1621 in Plymouth, Massachusetts, at the end of the harvest season, the Pilgrims and the Native Americans together celebrated a feast of thanksgiving. In a more formal way President George Washington in 1789 declared a National Day of Thanksgiving, which has been set now for the fourth Thursday in November.

The American bishops have approved a special set of readings and special Mass prayers to be used on this day. They can be found in the Lectionary and Sacramentary, and both highlight God's providential care of our country, symbolized by his care of his chosen people Israel. Both show God's infinite goodness and call us as a nation to share the blessings we have so richly received.

Reflections

---

## I.

*"It becomes us humbly to approach the throne of Almighty God, with gratitude and praise."*

As a special national holiday, a first motive of thanks is that requested by our founding fathers, who recognized God's special providence in the way so many people left situations in Europe of misery or persecution and found in the New World a place of freedom, abundance, and happiness. America was truly for them "the promised land."

This tradition has continued in our days with new waves of immigrants from Asia and Latin America seeking a share in the same blessings. This day should motivate us to be open to those new immigrants and help them find the same things our ancestors found here. Our national history and tradition has been one of welcome. On this day we give thanks for this dimension of our national history and pray that we continue to be a welcoming nation.

The Continental Congress in its Thanksgiving proclamation of 1779 highlighted this dimension:

> It becomes us humbly to approach the throne of Almighty God, with gratitude and praise for his goodness in conducting our forefathers to this western world; for his protection to them . . . for raising us, their children, from deep distress to be numbered among the nations of the earth.

As we celebrate the rich special blessings of our country on this day we should be even more motivated to show our gratitude by opening our hearts to concern for our fellow men and women at home and all over the globe so that in loving service we may share with them God's gifts to us.

## 2.

### *"Bless the LORD, O my soul!" (Ps 104:1)*

A second motive of thanksgiving today is provided by the fall harvest—a symbol of God's abundant goodness to us in nature. Often on this day a cornucopia of wheat, fruits, and vegetables is placed near the altar as a reminder of these gifts of God for the well-being of his children. If much of the year we take all this for granted, this special day is a good occasion for more conscious gratitude to a loving God for all these gifts of nature. A fitting prayer to use on this day is Psalm 104—"Bless the LORD, O my soul!"

When the Israelites first came into their promised land they expressed their gratitude for the fruits of the earth:

> When you have come into the land which the LORD, your God, is giving you as a heritage . . . you shall take some first fruits of the various products of the soil which you harvest from the land which the LORD, your God, gives you, and putting them in a basket, you shall go to the place the LORD, your God, chooses for the dwelling place of his name. . . . Then you shall declare before the LORD, your God . . . "[B]ringing us into this country, [the Lord] gave us this land flowing with milk and honey. Therefore, I have now brought you the first fruits of the products of the soil which you, O LORD, have given me." And having set them before the LORD, your God, you shall bow down in his presence. Then you and your family, together with the Levite and the aliens who live among you, shall make merry over all these good things which the LORD, your God, has given you. (Dt 26:1–11)

Again, our gratitude for the fruits of the earth implies a responsible sense of stewardship for that same earth. As believers we must be concerned not to spoil or ravage the good earth and environment God has given us. We must not use these resources in a selfish way that threatens future generations.

## 3.

*"Let the peace of Christ control your*
*hearts . . . and be thankful." (Col 3:15)*

Finally, it is very appropriate to celebrate this day as an occasion of deep personal gratitude to God for his rich blessings to us as individuals. In the words of today's Opening Prayer at Mass we are grateful that his "gifts of love are countless and his goodness is infinite."

Each of us might reflect today on some of those personal blessings and graces and offer our grateful praise to God. As a hymn often sung on this day says:

> Now thank we all our God with heart and hands and voices, Who wondrous things has done, in Whom His world rejoices; Who from our mother's arms has blessed us on our way with countless gifts of love and still is ours today.

Gratitude is an act of true contemplation and prayer that lifts us up beyond ourselves and our selfish pre-occupations to bask in the warmth of God's love and goodness. No wonder Paul urged the early Christians to "be thankful" (Col 3:15). Gratitude is a virtue by which we acknowledge in humility our total dependence on God, that he is the source of our life and all else.

A sign of the depth of our gratitude is to be grateful for everything—even blessings in disguise such as the setbacks and sufferings of life. A Trappist monk has written well of this dimension of thanksgiving:

> It is good to follow the old pious phrase about the adorable will of God, and unite the adoration of God to accepting His Holy Will, whatever it be. The AA prayer says it perfectly: "God grant me the serenity to accept the things I cannot change, courage to change the things

I can, and wisdom to know the difference." . . . There seems to be a time in God's plan that we may not take to. . . . If God wills it will come. We thank God, and we thank Him for everything. . . . Dorothy Day saw as much of the seamy side of life as many and far more than most. She asked for two words on her tombstone: Deo Gratias. Thanks be to God.[1]

# $\mathcal{O}$ur Lord Jesus Christ, King of the Universe

✤

## Historical Background

This feast is a relatively modern one. It was instituted in 1925 by Pope Pius XI on the occasion of that Jubilee Year. He asked that on this day each year the prayer of Consecration to Christ the King be recited publicly. The feast was originally scheduled on the last Sunday in October, as a Catholic counter to Reformation Sunday. Under Pope Paul VI's reform of the Roman calendar, the date of the feast was changed to the last Sunday of ordinary time.

The feast was begun during a period in which certain secular rulers were launching dictatorial regimes that would soon become diabolical vehicles of hatred and destruction. Through this feast, Pope Pius XI wanted to reassert the ultimate, universal sovereignty of Jesus Christ and his law of truth and love.

## Reflections

---

### I.

*"Jesus is Lord."*

While this feast is relatively modern, the acknowledgement of Jesus' absolute sovereignty goes back to the first Christian community. All that we mean by the word "King" is absorbed in the title "Lord," which the first Christians applied to Jesus. The first simple creed of the early Church was "Jesus is Lord":

> If you confess with your mouth that Jesus is Lord and believe in your heart that God raised him from the dead, you will be saved. . . . For the scripture says, "No one who believes in him will be put to shame." . . . For "everyone who calls on the name of the Lord will be saved." (Rom 10:9–13)

For the early Christians to say "Jesus is Lord" was an awesome faith declaration. The word they used was the same word the Greek Septuagint version of the Old Testament used for God. To say "Jesus is Lord" is to say "Jesus is God."[1] Therefore to Jesus there is accorded all the worship and homage one accords to God the Father:

> At the name of Jesus
> every knee should bend,
> of those in heaven and on earth and under the earth,
> and every tongue confess that
> Jesus Christ is Lord,
> to the glory of God the Father. (Phil 2:10–11)

The roots of Jesus' absolute Lordship and Kingship are found, as Pope Pius XI said in his apostolic letter instituting the feast, in his very being and nature, in what theologians call the "hypostatic union" of divinity and humanity in his one person:

As the Word of God, of one substance with the Father,
he must share in common with the Father all things.
Therefore he has absolute dominion over all created
things. (*Quas Primas*, 7)

As we acknowledge today Jesus as King we are but
echoing the faith and worship of the first Christians who
adored him as Lord. We recognize his supreme dominion
over all peoples. His is, as today's Preface notes, "an eternal
and universal kingdom: a kingdom of truth and life, a kingdom of holiness and grace, a kingdom of justice, love and
peace." The Church's mission is to make this dominion ever
more a reality among the peoples of our world.

## 2.

*"My kingdom does not belong to this world." (Jn 18:36)*

Jewish messianic expectation at Jesus' time was very much
centered on hope for a king, the promised descendent of
King David, the "perfect king" described in Psalm 72 used
in today's Office of Readings. This expectation complicated
Jesus' ministry. He was indeed a descendant of David, but
his view of his role was very different from that of the
crowd. "King" was not a title he was very comfortable with.
Indeed we read in John 6:15: "Since Jesus knew that they
were going to come and carry him off to make him king, he
withdrew again to the mountain alone."

Before Pilate, who asked, "Are you the King of the
Jews?" (Jn 18:33), Jesus, without denying his sovereign dignity, introduced a correction: "My kingdom does not
belong to this world" (v. 36) and went on to reveal his true
role as king of truth:

You say I am a king. For this I was born and for this I
came into the world, to testify to the truth. (Jn 18:37)

Jesus understands himself as Son, as obedient servant of
the Father—not as an earthly king. He comes to do the will
of the Father and empties himself in the humility of love; this

is who Jesus is, this is why he came! His subsequent exaltation by the Father was precisely in recognition and reward of his having lived this life of self-emptying obedience:

> Who, though he was in the form of God,
> did not regard equality with God something to be grasped.
> Rather, he emptied himself,
> taking the form of a slave,
> coming in human likeness;
> and found human in appearance,
> he humbled himself,
> becoming obedient to death,
> even death on a cross.
> Because of this, God greatly exalted him
> and bestowed on him the name
> that is above every name,
> that at the name of Jesus
> every knee should bend,
> of those in heaven and on earth and under the earth,
> and every tongue confess that
> Jesus Christ is Lord,
> to the glory of God the Father. (Phil 2:6–11)

## 3.

### *"O Lord—come!"*

Today is also a "feast of hope." Jesus, our Lord and King, is now "in the glory of God the Father"—he sits forever in victorious triumph at the right hand of God. He has definitively overcome evil, sin, and death: "The LORD is king, in splendor robed," as Psalm 93 says (v. 1). We rejoice today that he is forever "King of Kings and Lord of Lords."

In glory he has not abandoned us, but is our great Advocate and High Priest—ever interceding for us with the Father. Moreover, we look for Christ the King to come again in glory. As we have noted earlier, the prayer of the early Christians was *Marana tha*, "O Lord—come!" (1 Cor 16:22).

Christ will return one day to bring human history with all its grandeur and misery to a definitive conclusion. His cause will be vindicated and his faithful disciples rewarded. The powerful imagery of the Book of Revelation evokes this grand finale:

> Sitting on a cloud [was] one who looked like a son of a man, with a gold crown on his head and a sharp sickle in his hand. Another angel came out of the temple, crying out in a loud voice to the one sitting on the cloud, "Use your sickle and reap the harvest, for the time to reap has come." (Rev 14:14–15)

We can live in hope if we know that all things will be made right. Christ's sovereignty will be definitively established one day and all people will be subjected to his most gentle rule, which will last forever. Until that day comes, we must be faithful and wait for him with hope.

# Notes

## Advent

1. Thomas J. Talley, *The Origins of the Liturgical Year* (New York: Pueblo Publishing, 1986), 79.
2. Ibid.,150.
3. Pierre Teilhard de Chardin, *The Divine Milieu* (New York: Harper and Row, 1960), 151–152.

## Immaculate Conception of Mary

1. Christopher O' Donnell, *At Worship with Mary* (Wilmington, DE: Michael Glazier Co, 1998), 213 ff.
2. Joseph Gerry, *Ever Present Lord* (Petersham, MA: St Bede's Publications, 1989), 27.

## Our Lady of Guadalupe

1. Luis Medina Ascensio, *The Apparitions of Guadalupe* (Washington DC: A CARA Publication, 1980).
2. *L'Osservatore Romano*, January 25, 1982.
3. Augustine Di Noia, O.P., "Our Lady of Guadalupe," *Magnificat*, 2007, 166.

## Nativity of Our Lord: Christmas

1. Romano Guardini, *The Lord* (Chicago: Regnery Co., 1954), 15.
2. Pope Benedict XVI, *Deus Caritas Est*, 1.
3. Pope Benedict XVI, General Audience Address, December 20, 2006.
4. Avery Cardinal Dulles, S.J., "Incarnation," *Commonweal*, Dec. 28, 1973, 336.

## Epiphany of Our Lord

1. Karl Rahner, *The Eternal Year* (Montreal: Palm Publishers, 1964), 42–46.
2. Ian Ker, *Newman: On Being a Christian* (Notre Dame, IN: University of Notre Dame Press, 1990), 74.

## Presentation of the Lord

1. Blessed Guerric of Igny [Cistercian Abbot, 1087–1157], *Liturgical Sermons* (Shannon, Ireland: Irish University Press, 1970), 100.
2. Augustine Di Noia, O.P., "The Hope of the Presentation," *Magnificat*, February 2006, 39–40.

## Lent

1. Talley, *The Origins of the Liturgical Year,* 165.
2. Thomas Merton, *Seasons of Celebration* (New York: Farrar, Straus and Giroux, 1965), 137.
3. Rahner, *The Eternal Year,* 66–68.
4. Cited in Joseph Gerry, *Ever Present Lord* (Petersham, MA: St. Bede Publications, 1989), 105.

## St. Joseph, Husband of Mary

1. Joseph Cardinal Ratzinger, *Co-Workers of the Truth* (San Francisco: Ignatius Press, 1992), 94–95.

## Annunciation of the Lord

1. Frederick Faber, *Bethlehem* (New York: Catholic Publication Society, 1860), 53.
2. Rev. Dominic Whedbee, O.C.S.O., Homily, St Joseph's Abbey, Spencer, MA, March 25, 2004.
3. Guerric of Igny, *Liturgical Sermons* (Kalamazoo, MI: Cistercian Publications, 1971), 32–33.
4. Bernard of Clairvaux, Homily 4, cited in *The Liturgy of the Hours* (New York: Catholic Book Publishing Co., 1975), 1:345.

## Sunday of the Lord's Passion: Palm Sunday

1. Henri J.M. Nouwen, *The Road to Daybreak* (New York: Doubleday, 1988). Quoted in *Eternal Seasons* (Notre Dame, IN: Sorin Books, 2004), 100.
2. Pope Paul VI, Palm Sunday Homily, 1977.
3. Pope Benedict XVI, Palm Sunday Homily, 2006.
4. Archbishop Oscar Romero, Palm Sunday Homily, 1978.

## Easter

1. Talley, *The Origins of the Liturgical Year,* 1–6.
2. Gerald O'Collins, *Interpreting the Resurrection* (New York: Paulist Press, 1998).
3. Rahner, *The Eternal Year,* 82–88.
4. Eduardo Cardinal Pironio, "In the Joy of Paschal Newness," *L'Osservatore Romano,* May 26, 1977.

## Ascension of the Lord

1. Angelo Amato, *Gesu` Il Signore* (Bologna: Dehoniane Edizione, 1999), 556.

2.  Ibid., 560.

3.  Rahner, *The Eternal Year*, 97.

4.  Pope Benedict XVI, Ascension Homily, May 7, 2005, *L'Osservatore Romano*, May 11, 2005.

### Pentecost

1.  Guerric of Igny, *Liturgical Sermons*, 109.

2.  Rahner, *The Eternal Year*, 106.

### Trinity Sunday

1.  Prosper Gueranger, *The Liturgical Year*, vol. 10 (Dublin: Duffy and Sons, 1879), 109ff.

2.  Augustine, *The Trinity* (Brooklyn: New City Press, 1990), bk. VIII, chap. 5, #14.

3.  Ibid., # 12

4.  Henri J. M. Nouwen, *Behold the Beauty of the Lord* (Notre Dame, IN: Ave Maria Press, 1987, 2007), 32.

5.  Hans Urs von Balthasar, *You Crown the Year* (San Francisco: Ignatius Press, 1989), 144.

6.  Gueranger, 136ff.

### Body and Blood of the Lord

1.  Gueranger, *The Liturgical Year*, vol. 10, 150ff.

2.  Nouwen, *The Road to Daybreak*. Quoted in *Eternal Seasons*, 145–146.

3.  Rahner, *The Eternal Year*, 114ff.

### Sacred Heart of Jesus

1.  Cited in *Praying to Our Lord Jesus Christ*, ed. Benedict J. Groeschel (San Francisco: Ignatius Press, 2004), 31.

2.  Cited in *Magnificat*, June 2006.

3.  Fr. James Palmigiano, O.C.S.O., Homily on Sacred Heart, 2004, St. Joseph's Abbey, Spencer, MA.

### Nativity of John the Baptist

1.  Matthew Kelty, O.C.S.O., *Gethsemani Homilies* (Quincy, IL: Franciscan Press, 2001), 108–109.

### Transfiguration of Our Lord

1.  Carroll Stuhlmueller, *Biblical Meditations for Ordinary Time: Weeks 10–22* (New York: Paulist Press, 1984), 409.

2. Karl Rahner, *The Great Church Year* (New York: Crossroad, 1993), 340–342.

## Assumption of the Blessed Virgin Mary

1. See Stephen Shoemaker, *Ancient Traditions of the Virgin Mary's Dormition and Assumption* (New York: Oxford University Press, 2002) and Kilian Healy, *The Assumption of Mary* (Wilmington, DE: Michael Glazier, Inc., 1982).

## Nativity of the Blessed Virgin Mary

1. Guardini, *The Lord*, 7.
2. Guerric of Igny, *Liturgical Sermons* (Spencer, MA: Cistercian Publications, 1971), 192.

## Archangels Michael, Gabriel, Raphael, and All the Angels

1. John Cardinal Wright, "Some Reflection on the Angels," *L'Osservatore Romano*, July 6, 1972, 6–8.
2. Yves Congar, O.P., "On the Holy Angels," in *Faith and Spiritual Life* (New York: Herder and Herder, 1968), 18.

## All Saints

1. J.H. Newman, "Feast of All Saints," in *Parochial and Plain Sermons* (San Francisco: Ignatius Press, 1987), 478.
2. All of chapter 5 of *Lumen Gentium* on the "Call to Holiness" would be a fitting reading on this day.
3. John Cardinal Wright, "The Church of the Saints," in *The Saints Always Belong to the Present* (San Francisco: Ignatius Press, 1985), 42.

## Thanksgiving Day

1. Kelty, O.C.S.O., *Gethsemani Homilies*, 25.

## Our Lord Jesus Christ, King of the Universe

1. Larry Hurtado, *Lord Jesus Christ: Devotion to Jesus in Earliest Christianity* (Grand Rapids, MI: Eerdmans Press, 2003), see pp. 79–151.

MSGR. FRANCIS D. KELLY, a priest of the Diocese of Worcester, Massachusetts, is Superior of Casa Santa Maria, the house for English-speaking priests pursuing graduate studies in Rome. Prior to beginning this ministry in 2005, he served as Rector of Blessed John XXIII National Seminary in Weston, MA. From 1979–1992, he was Executive Director of the Department of Religious Education at the National Catholic Educational Association, and he previously served as Diocesan Director of Religious Education in Worcester.

❧